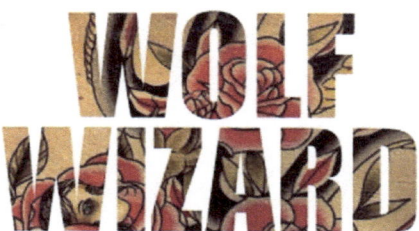

Note* *Please only use this book as a reference to inspire ideas and **do not copy** and tattoo these images.*

Wolf Wizard Press©
150 Ridge Street
Reno, NV 89509

Edited by: Jason Freeman

jfreemantattoo

Made in the USA.

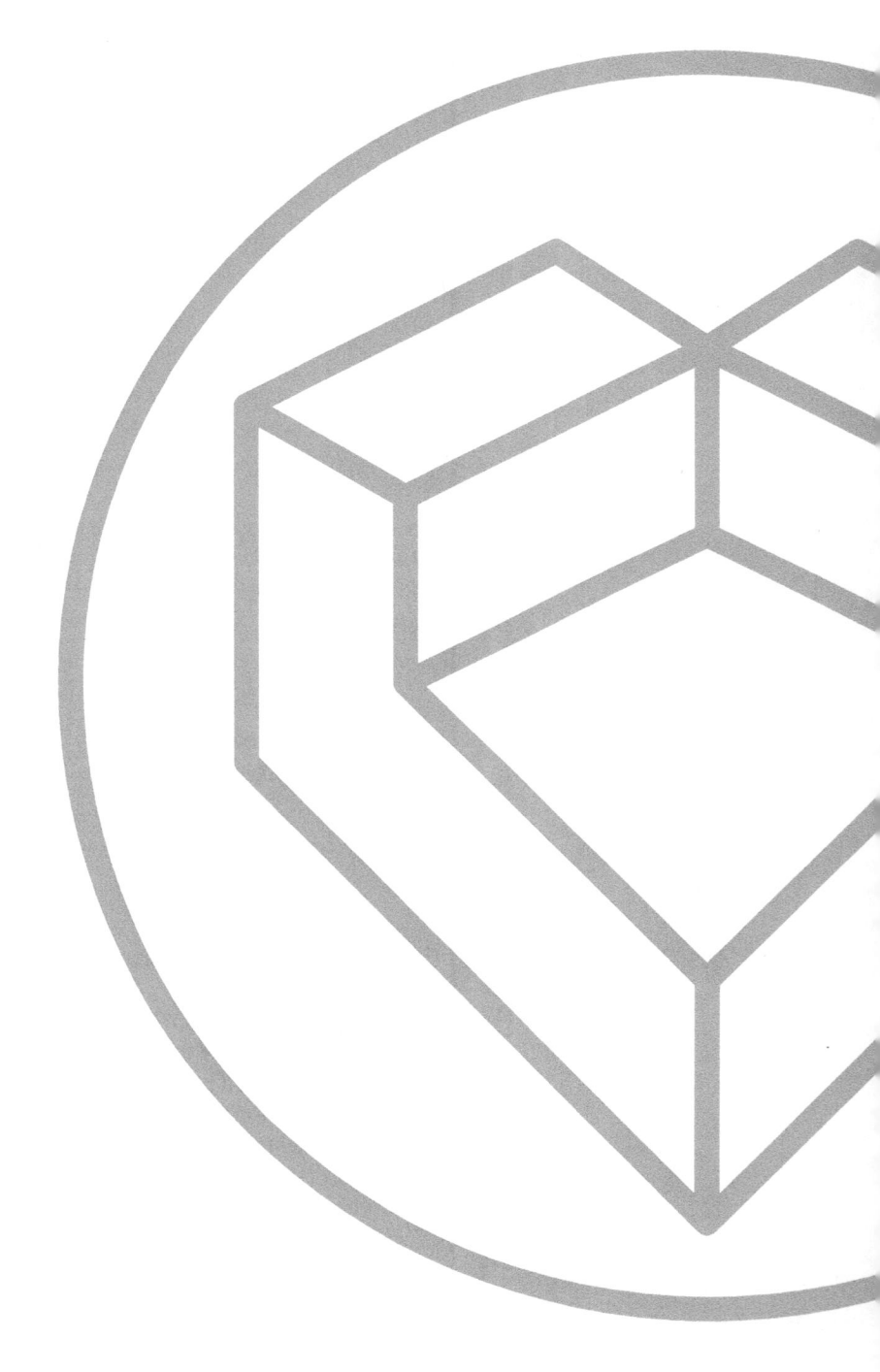

Table of Contents

Page #

Adam Warmerdam

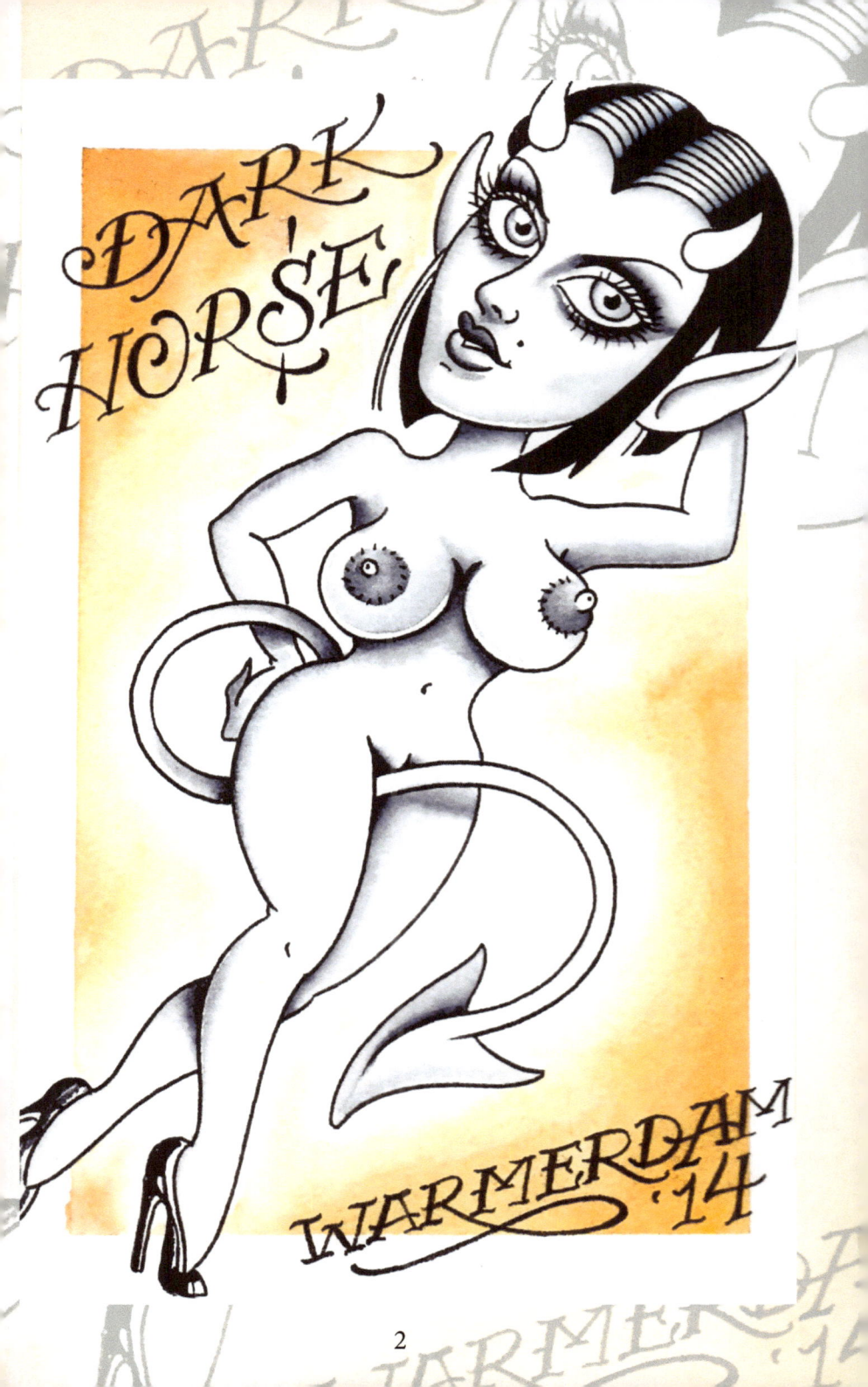

ADRIAN SANCHEZ

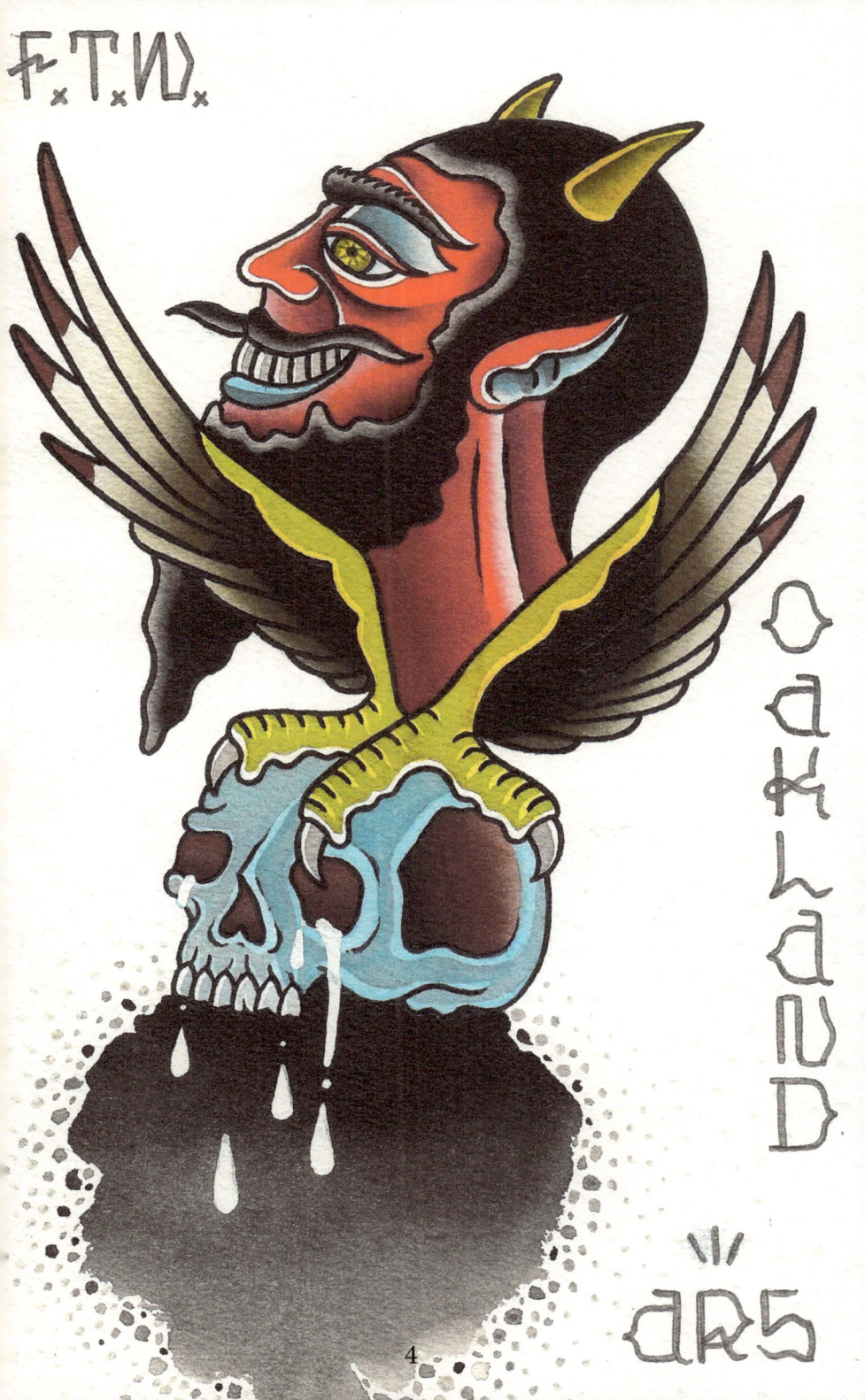

ANDY CHISM

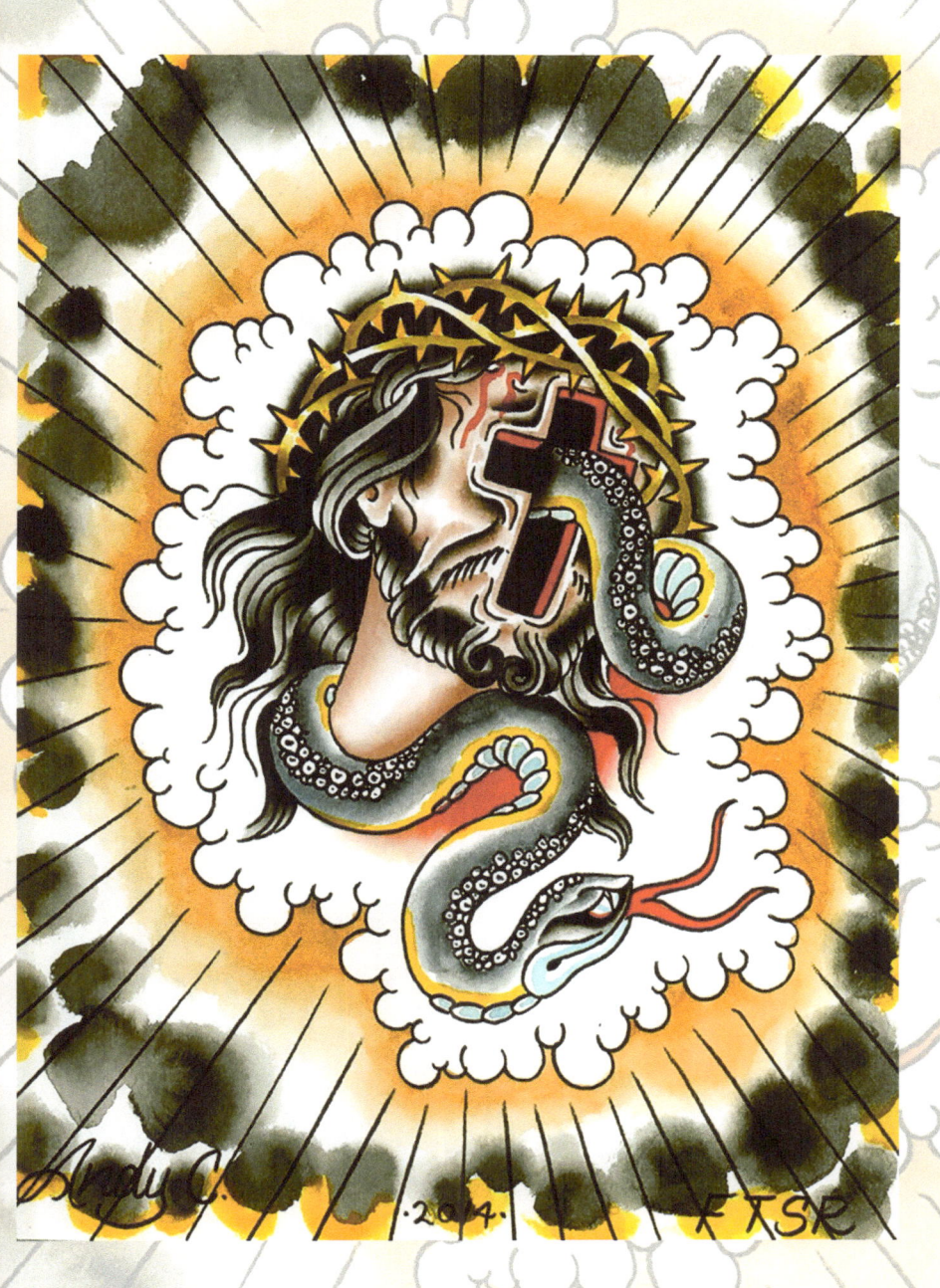

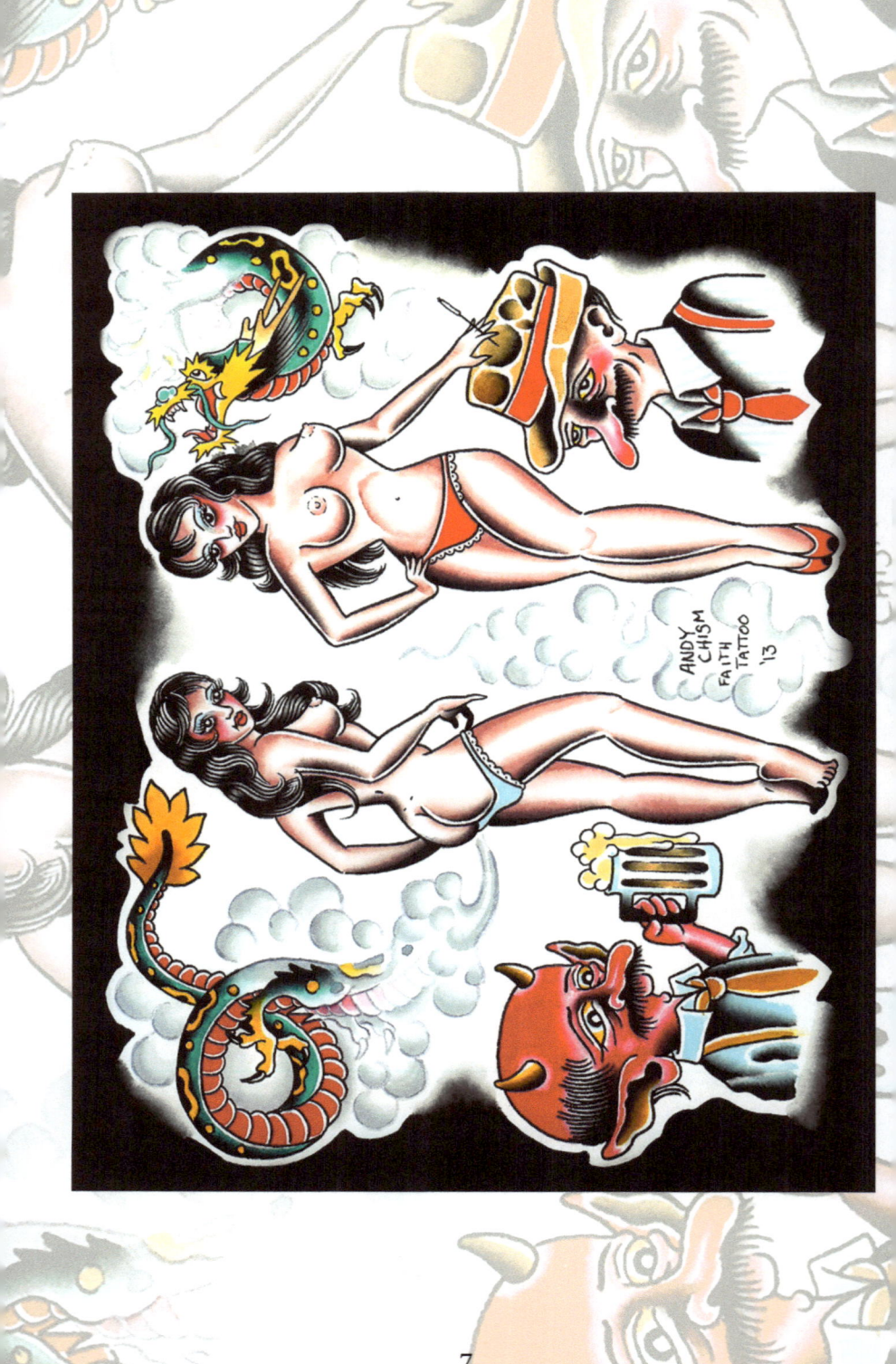

7

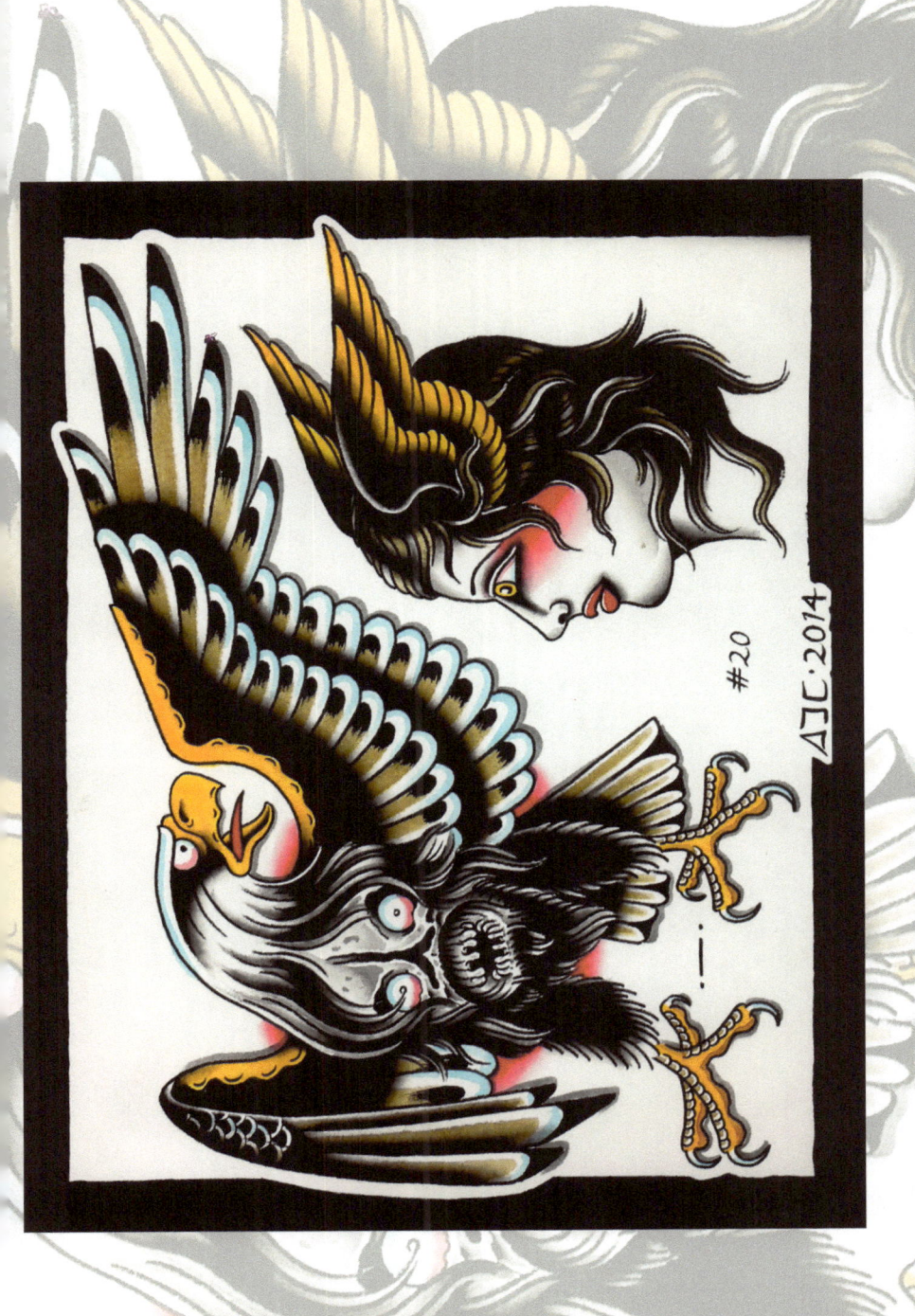

8

BEN CHEESE

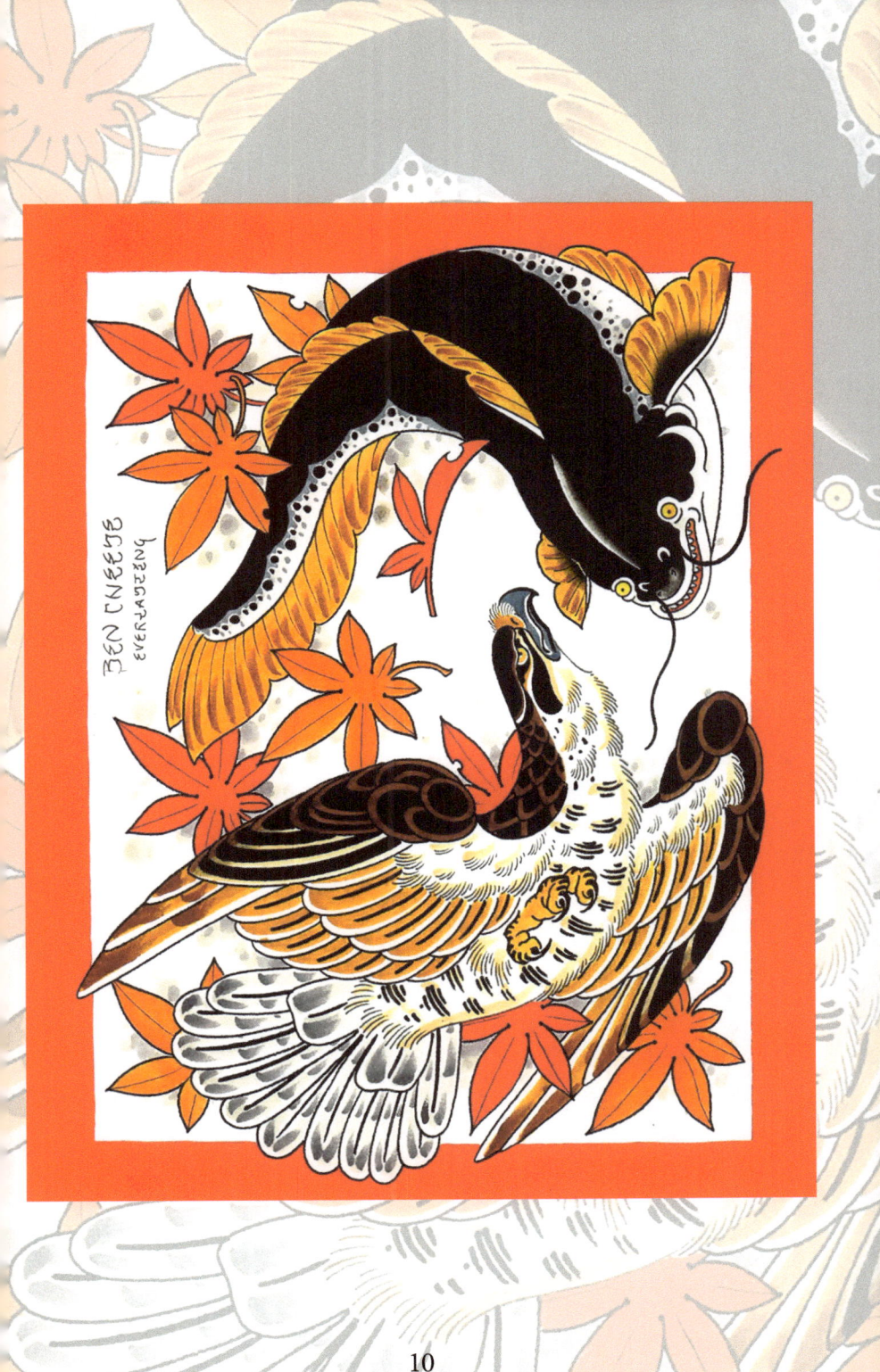

CASEY COKRLIC

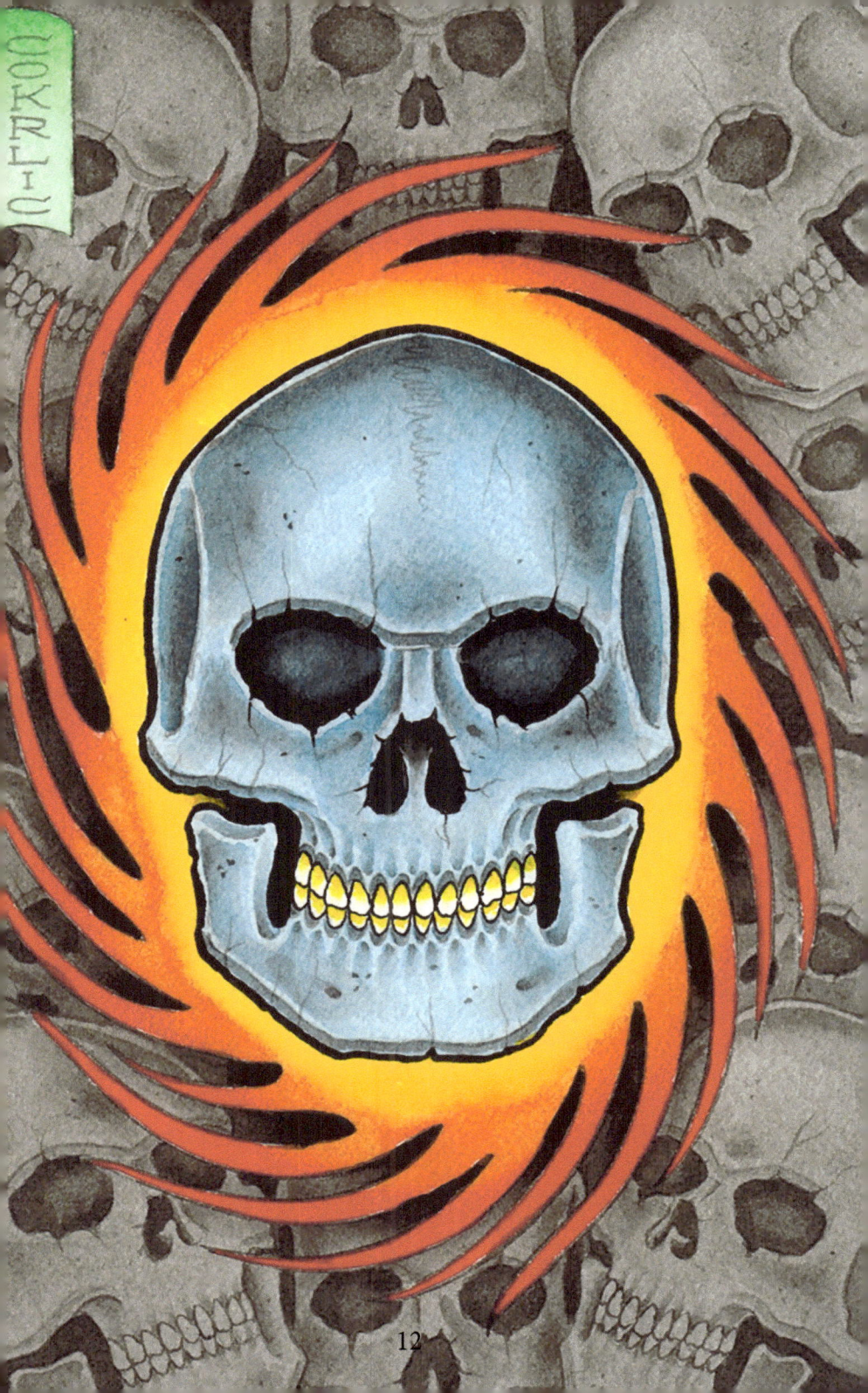

12

CHAD CLARK

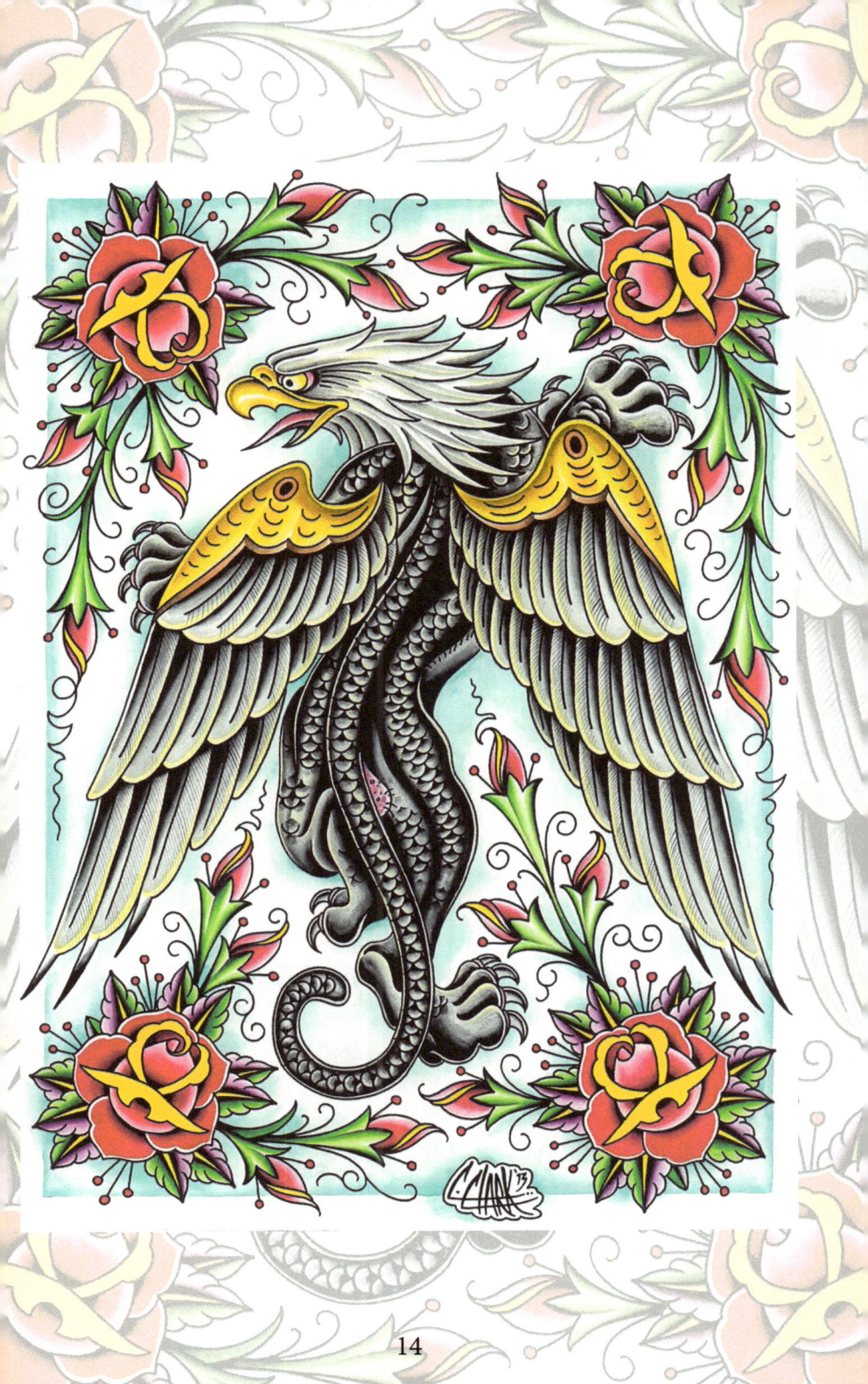

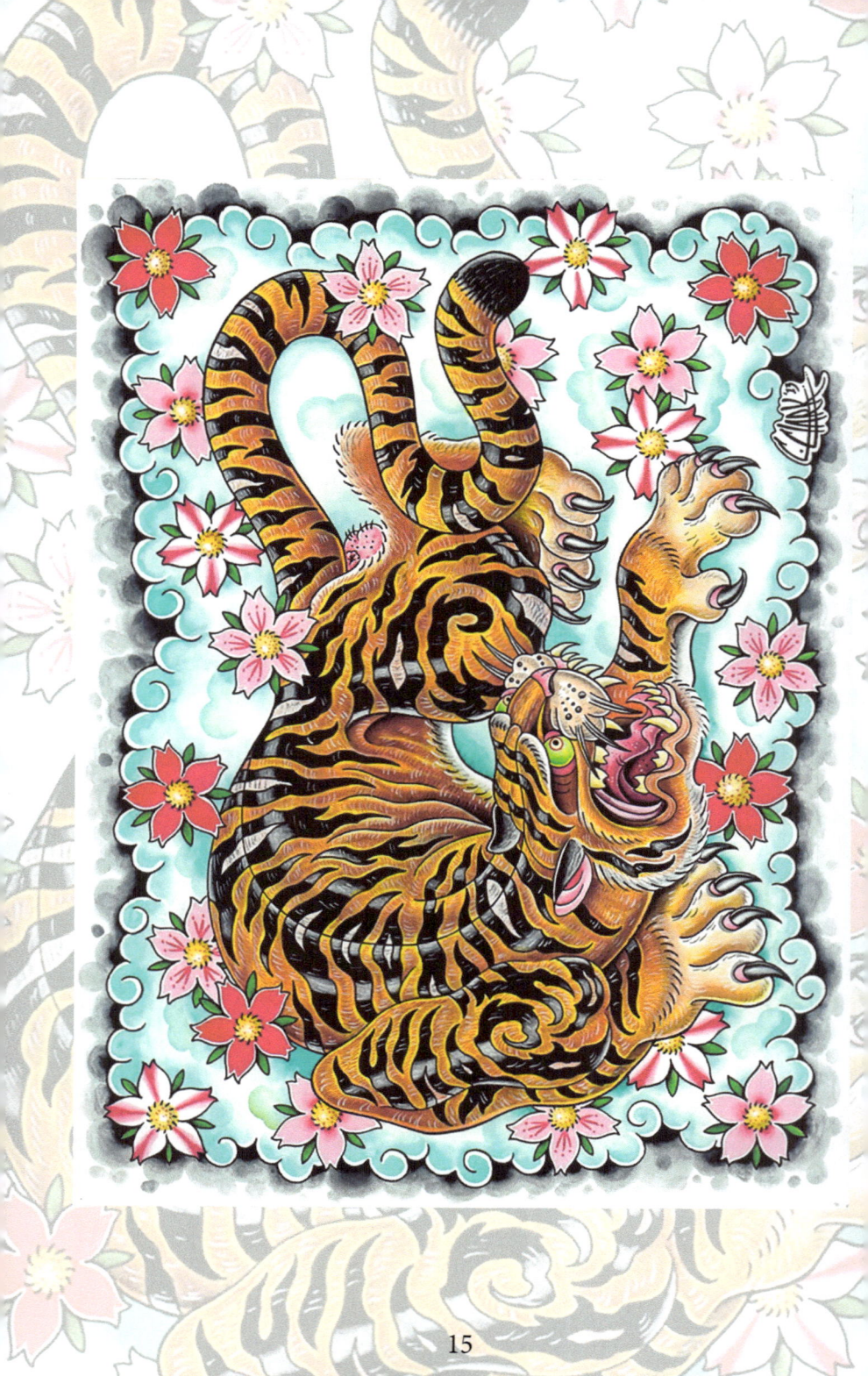

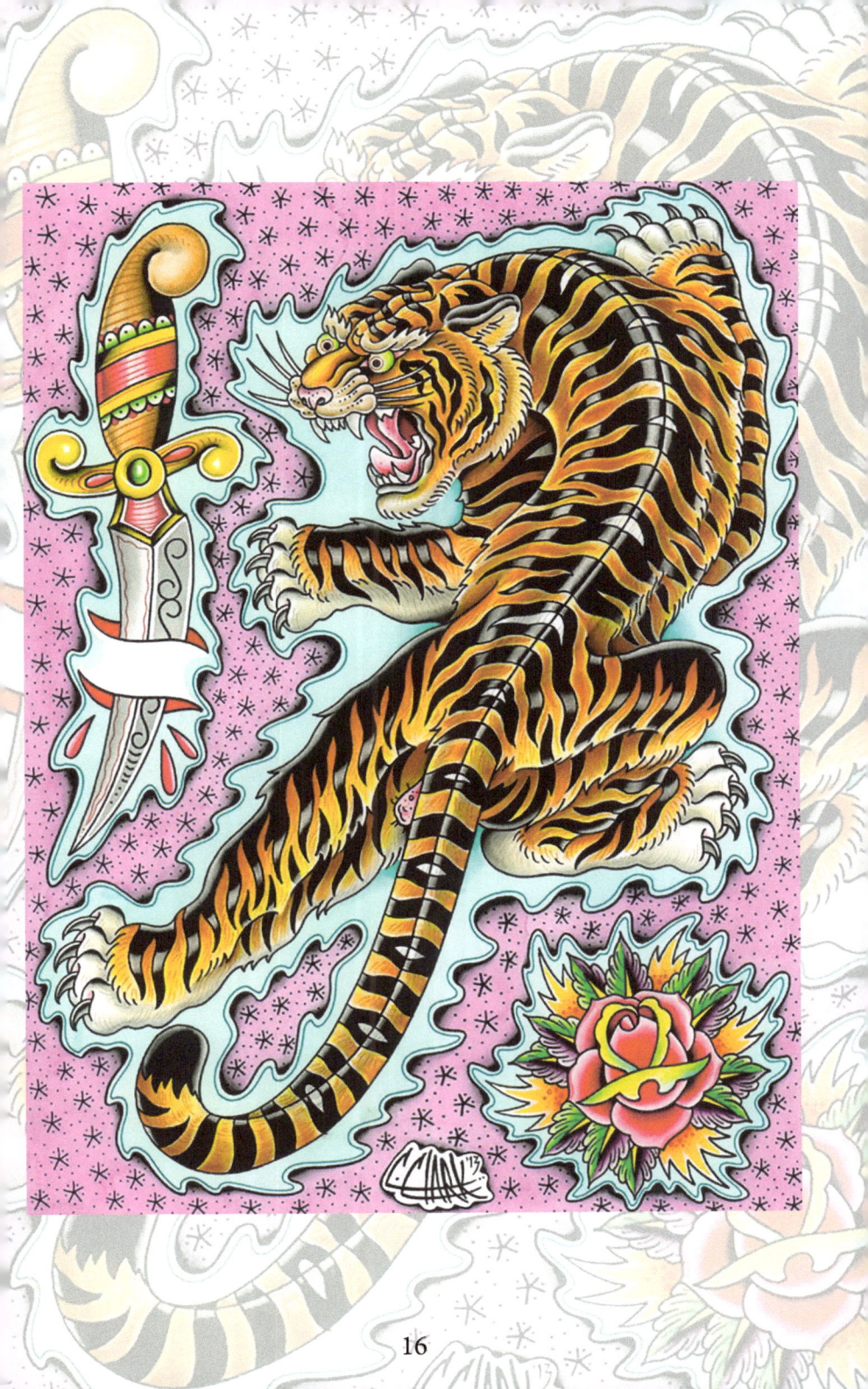

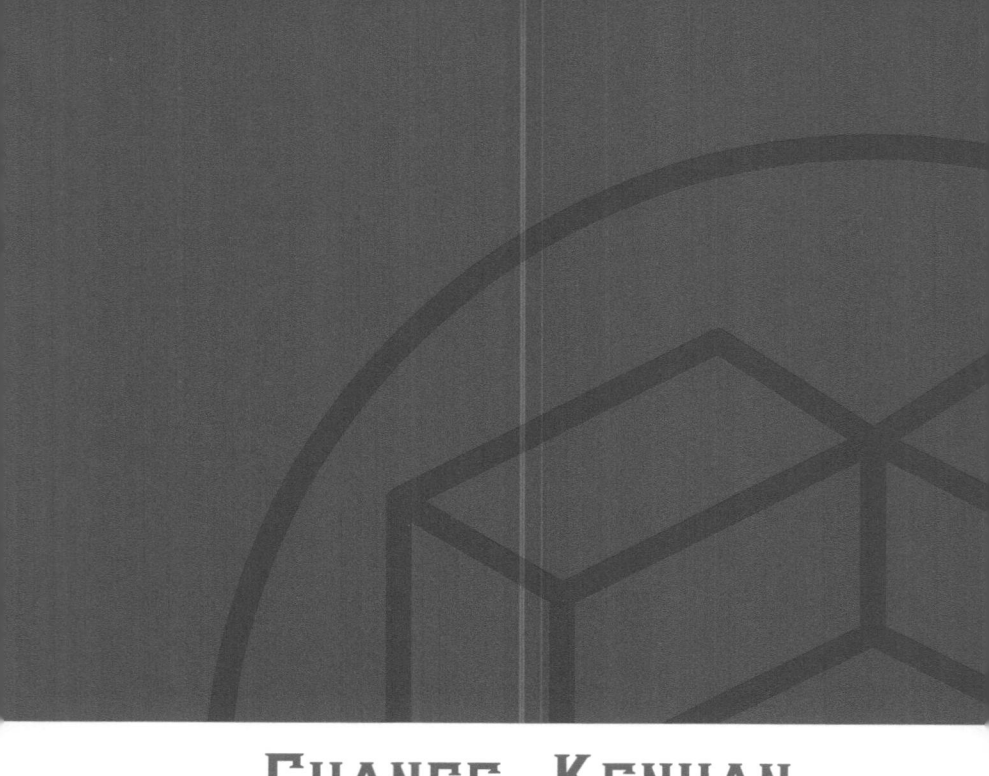

CHANGE KENYAN

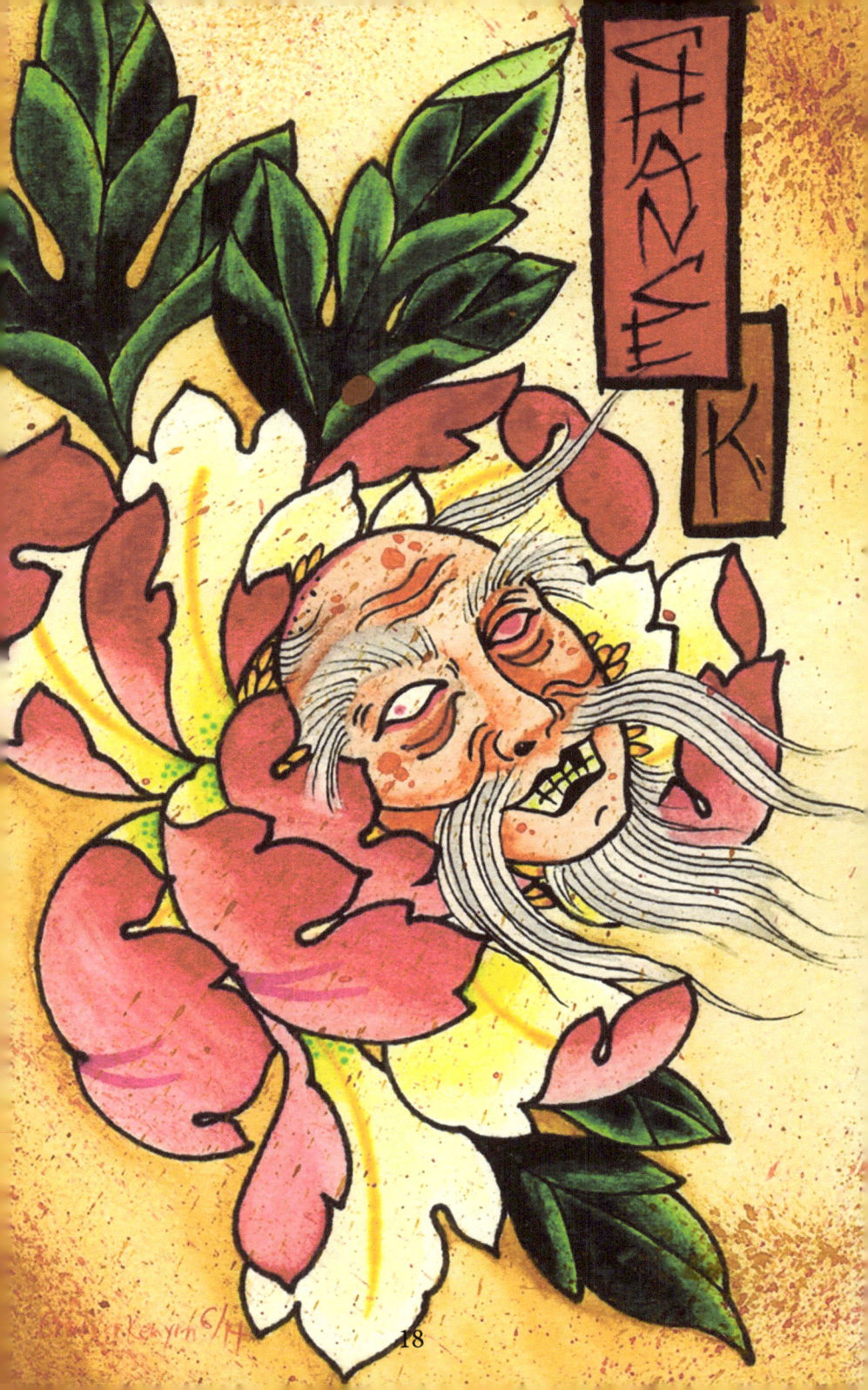

18

CHRIS LUDOVINA

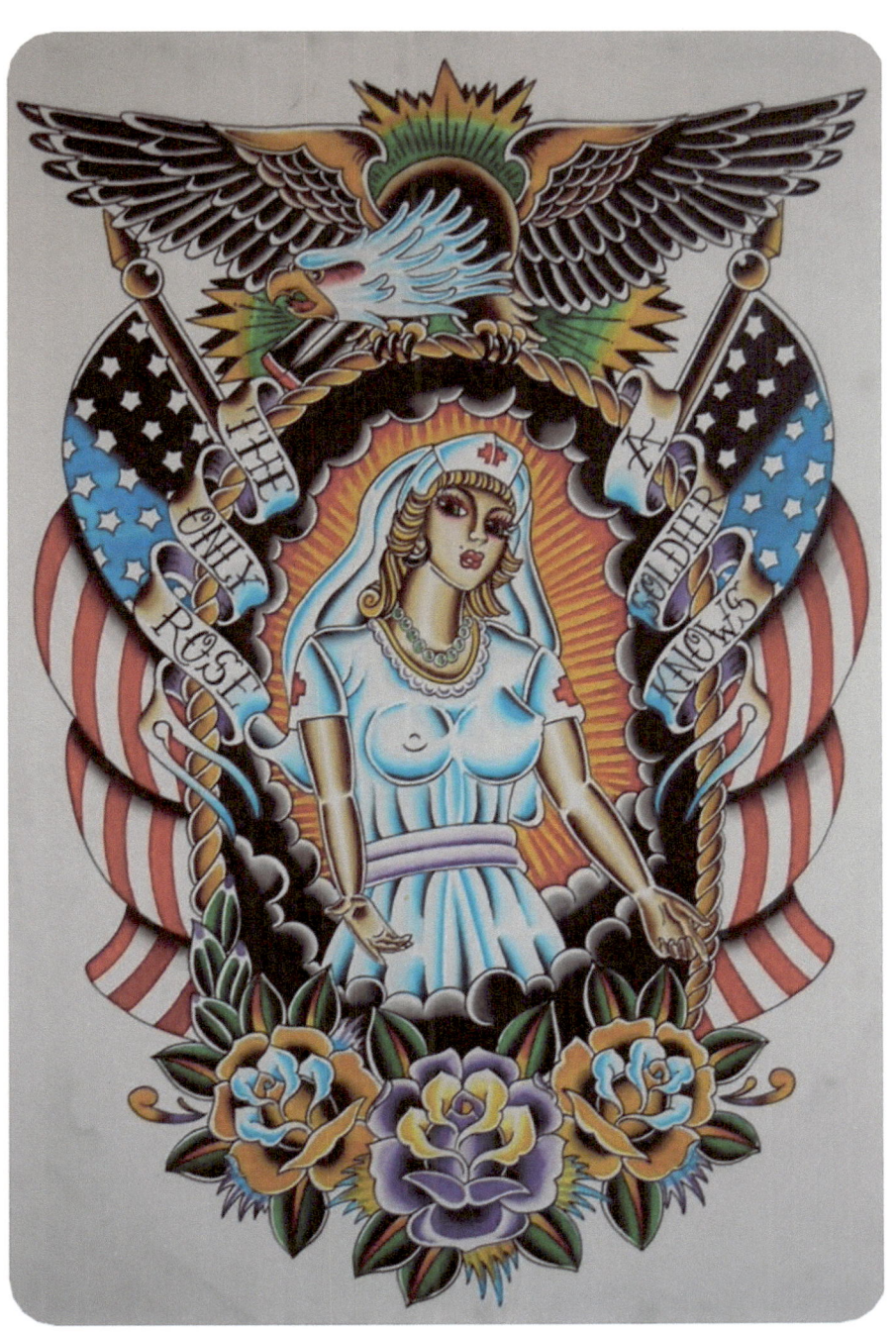

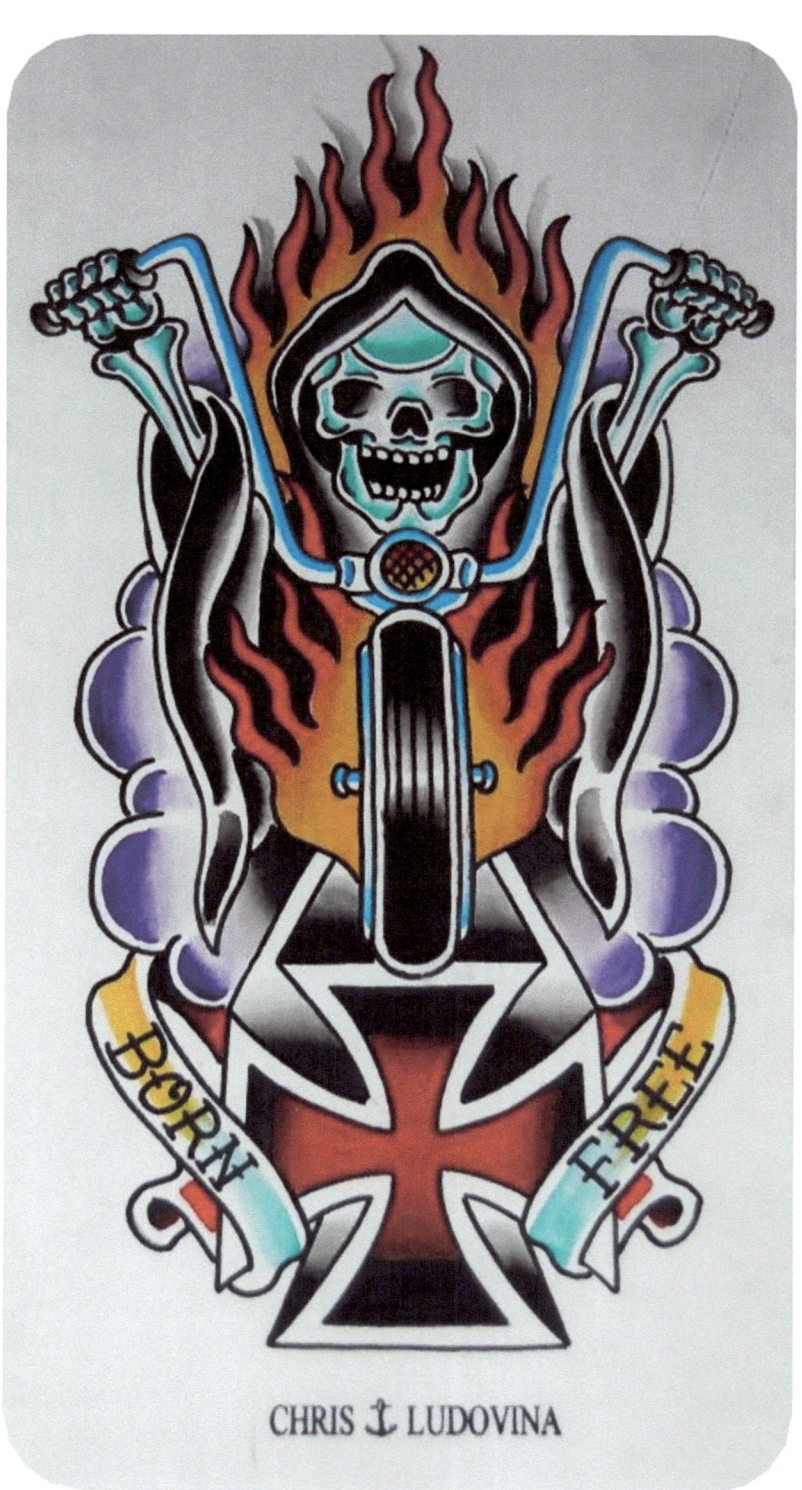

CHRIS ⚓ LUDOVINA

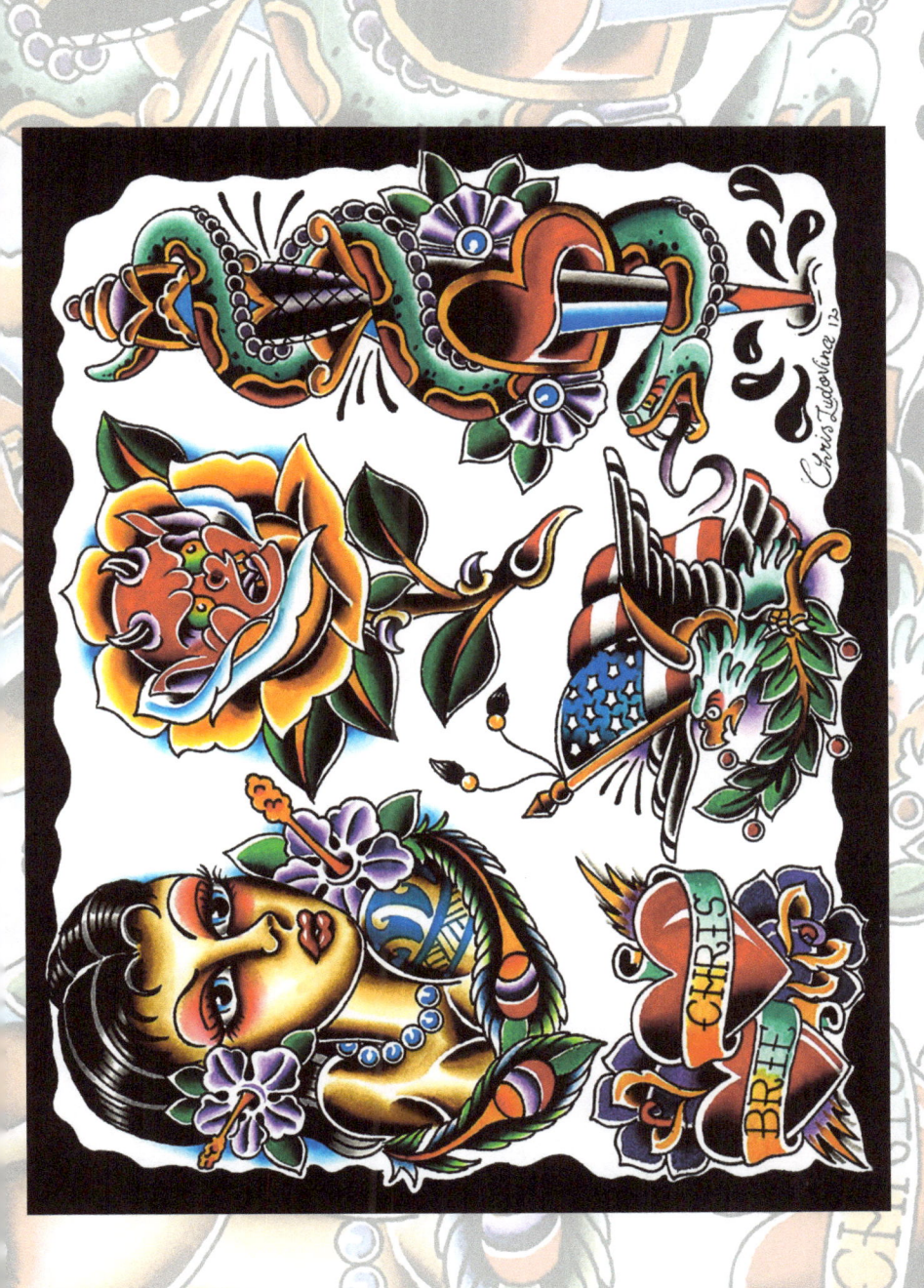

DEREK NOBLE

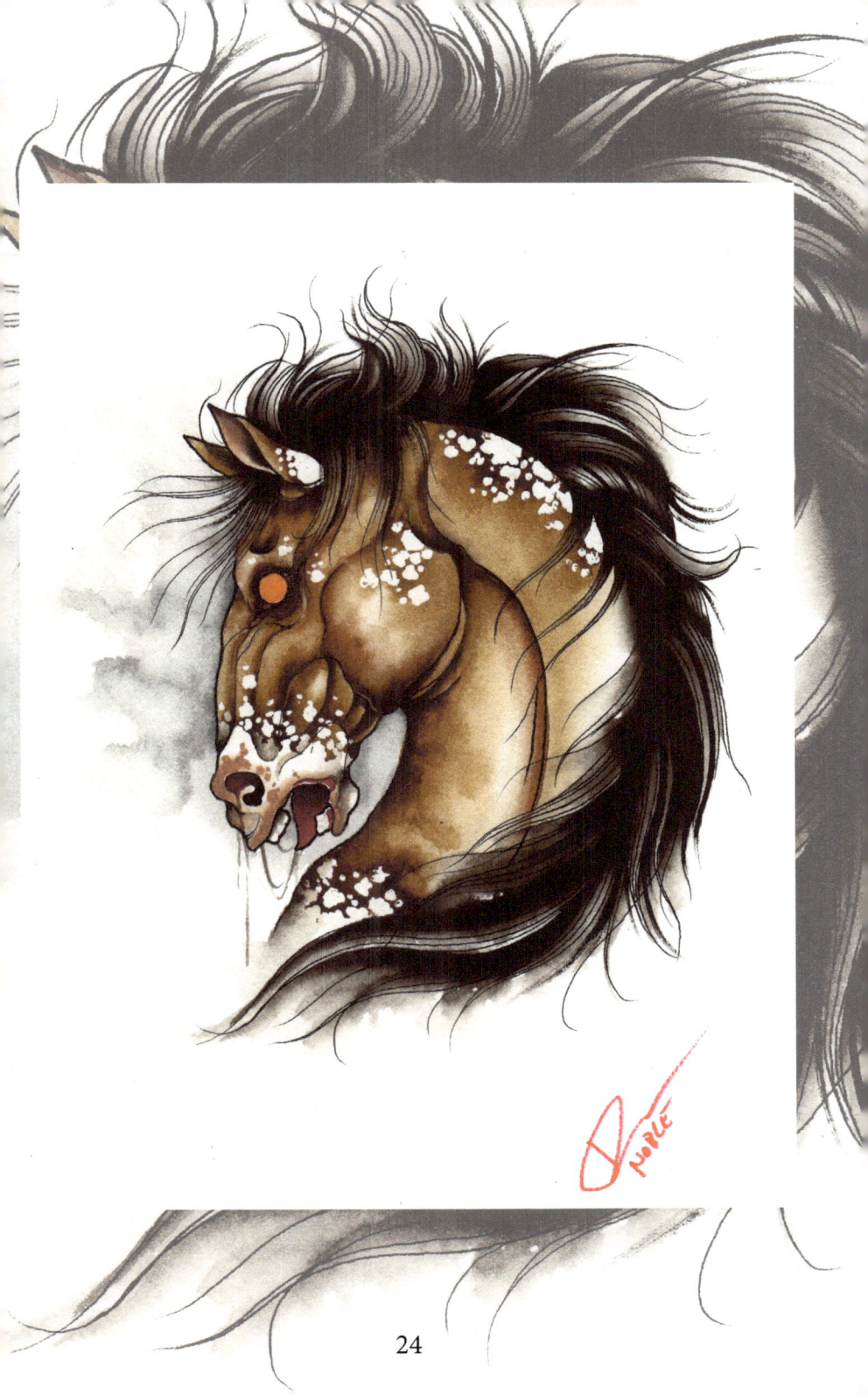

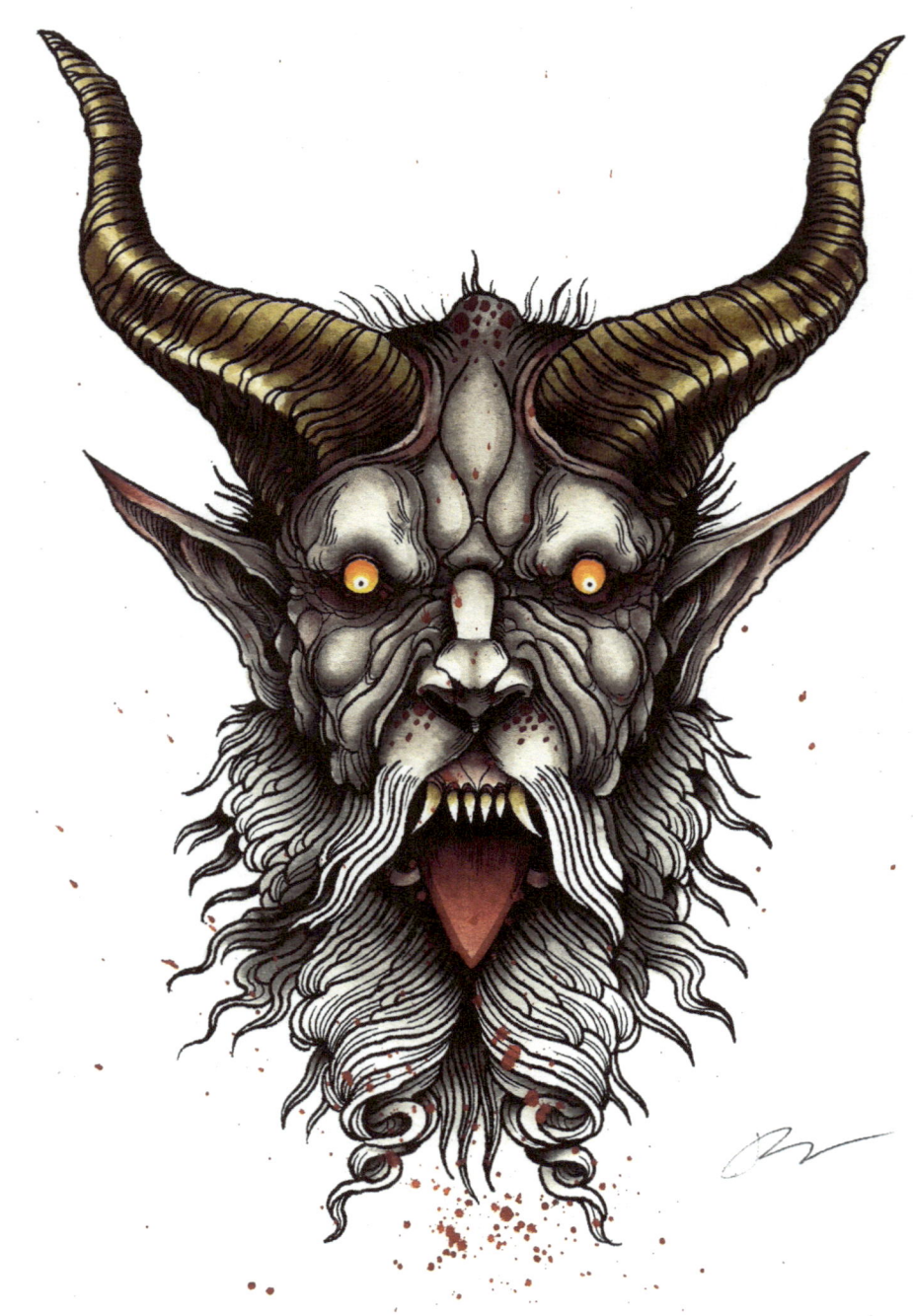

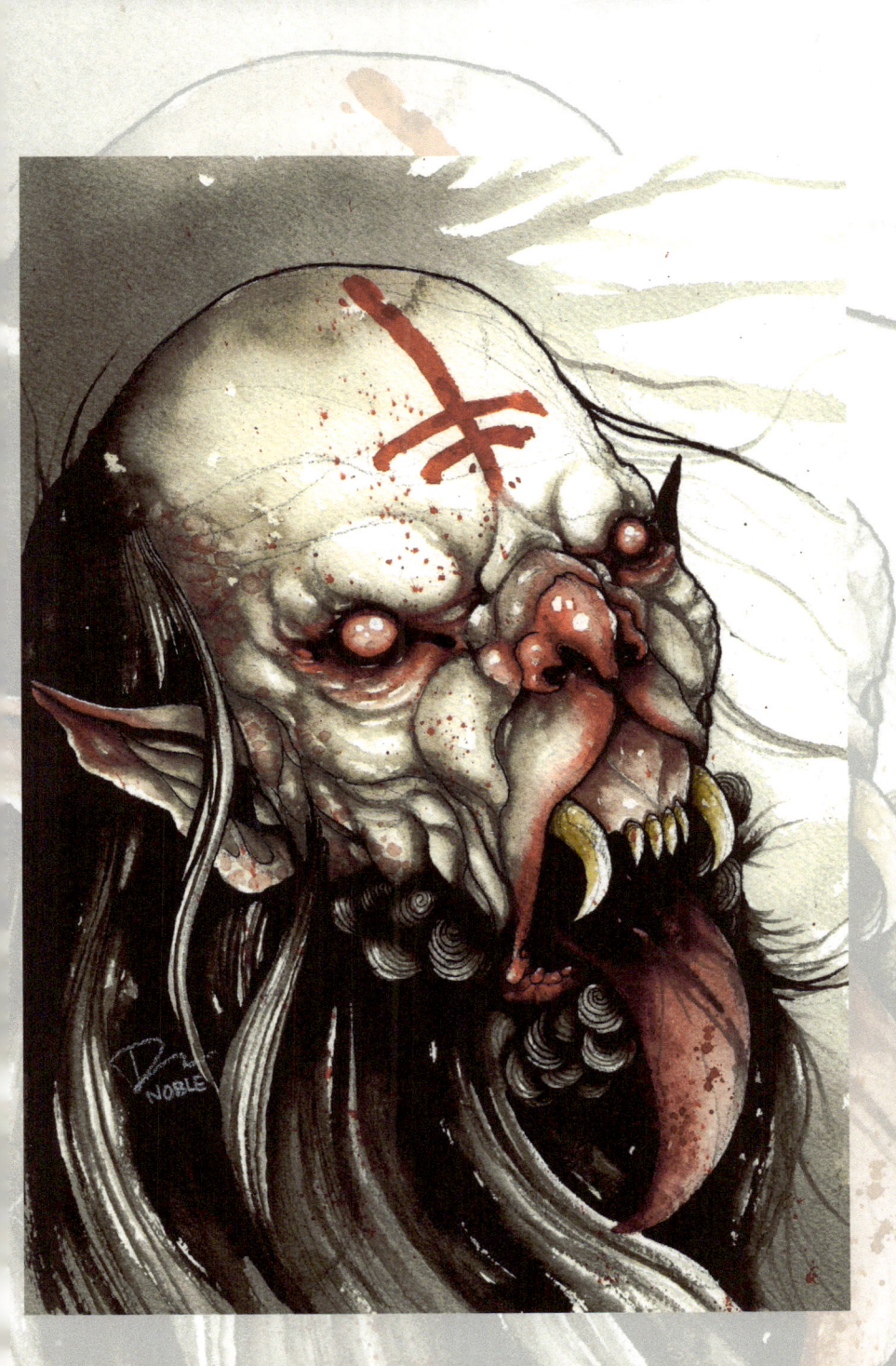

DRU BIAS

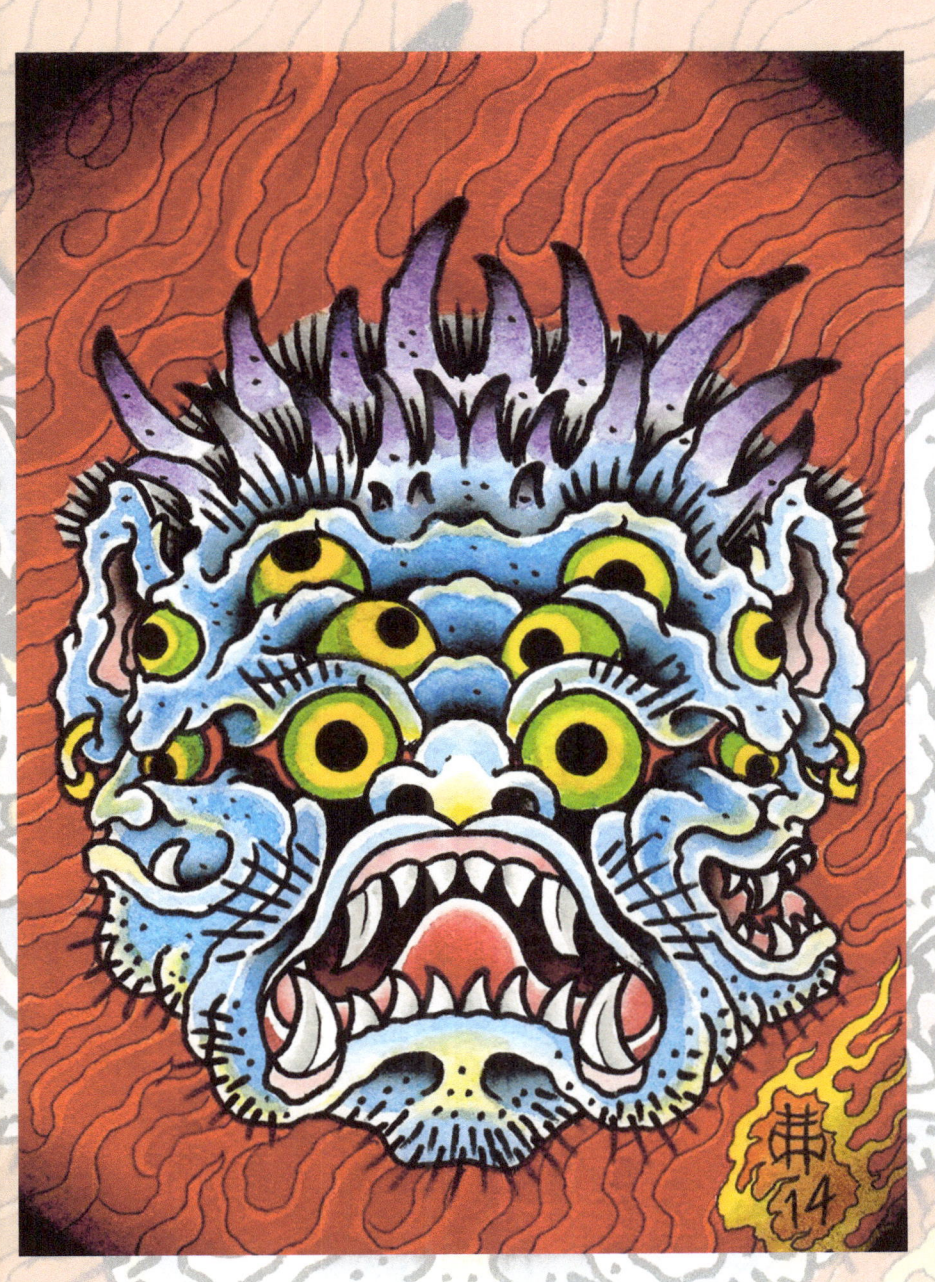

28

GREG HOWELL

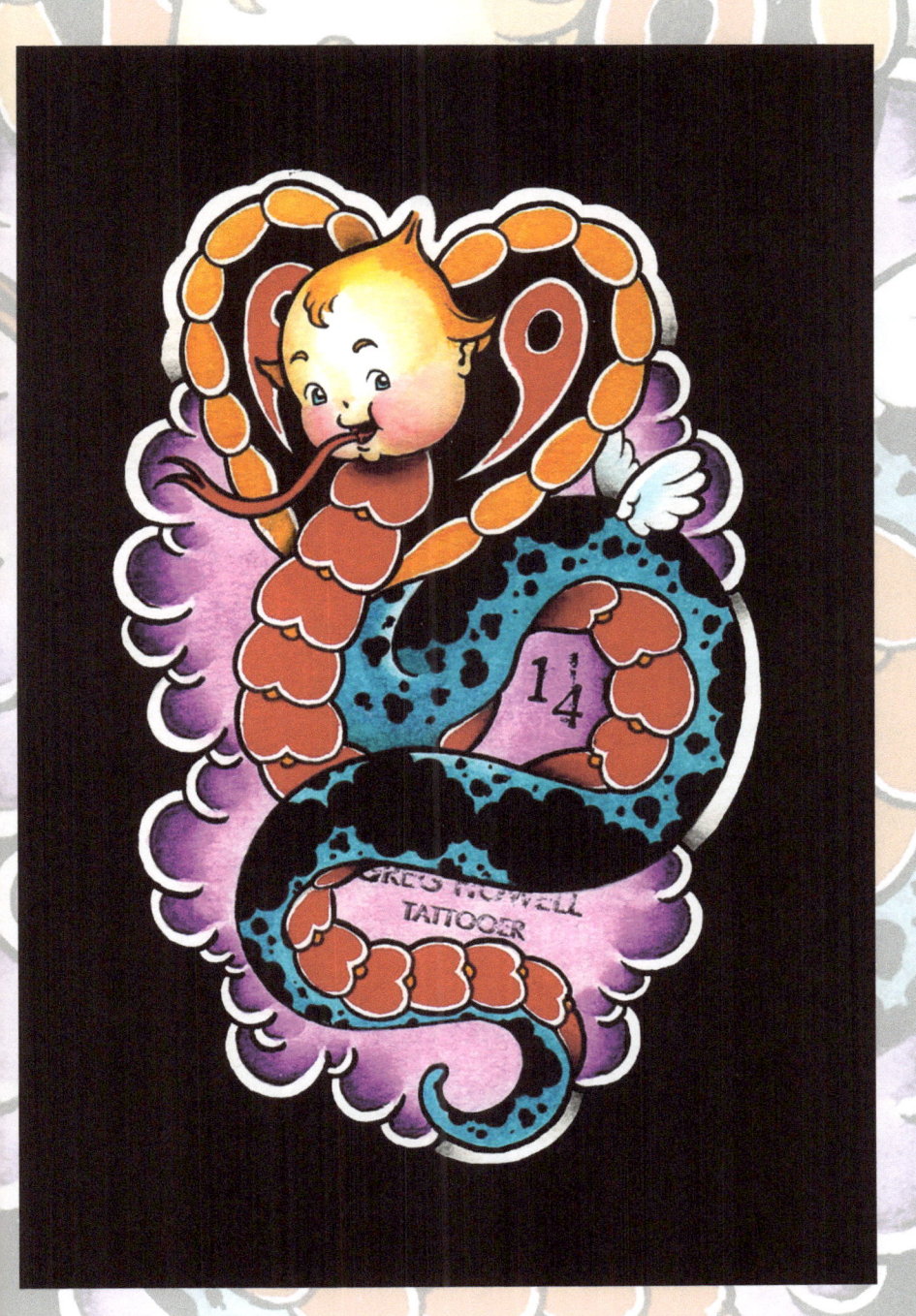

30

JASON FREEMAN

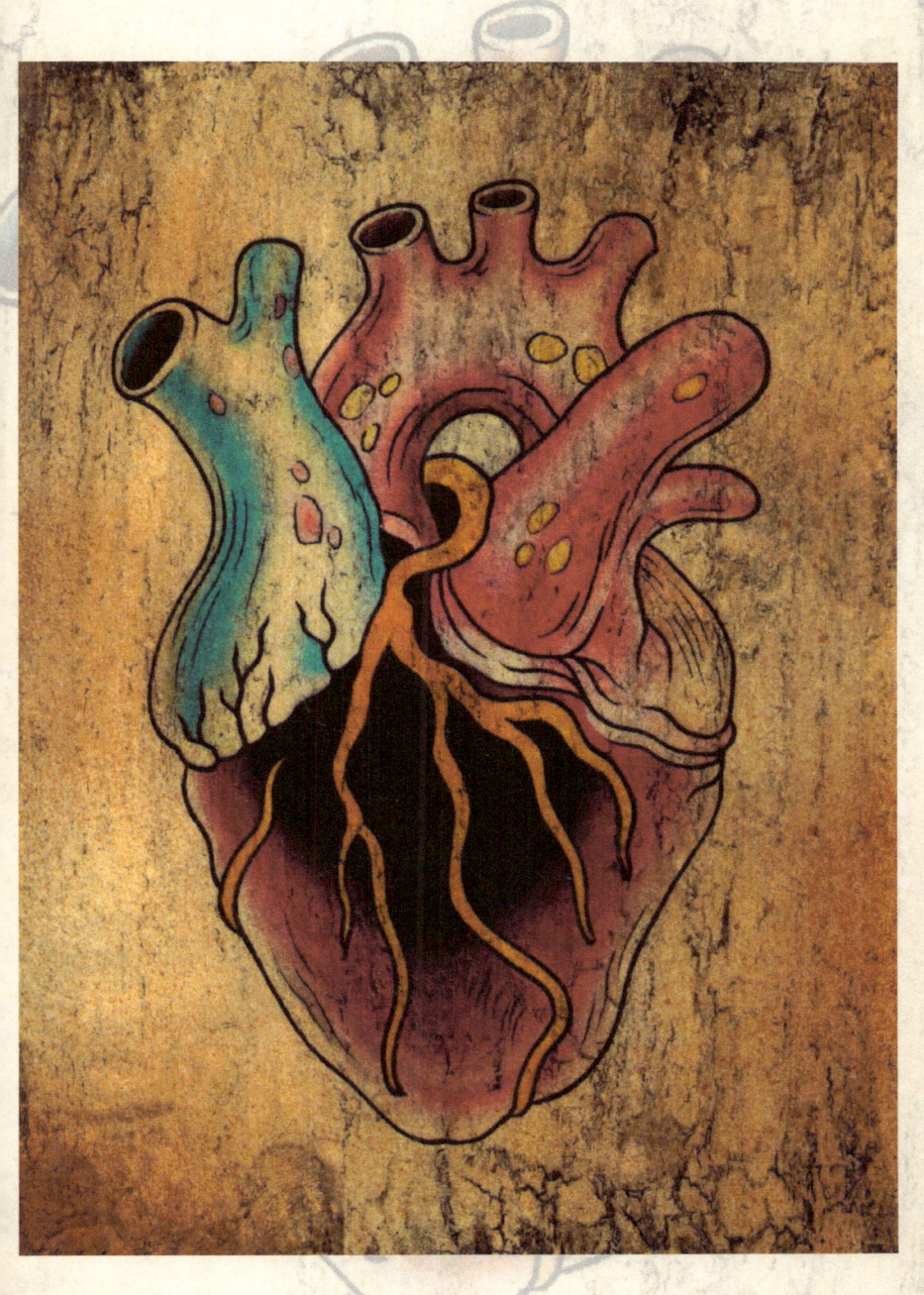

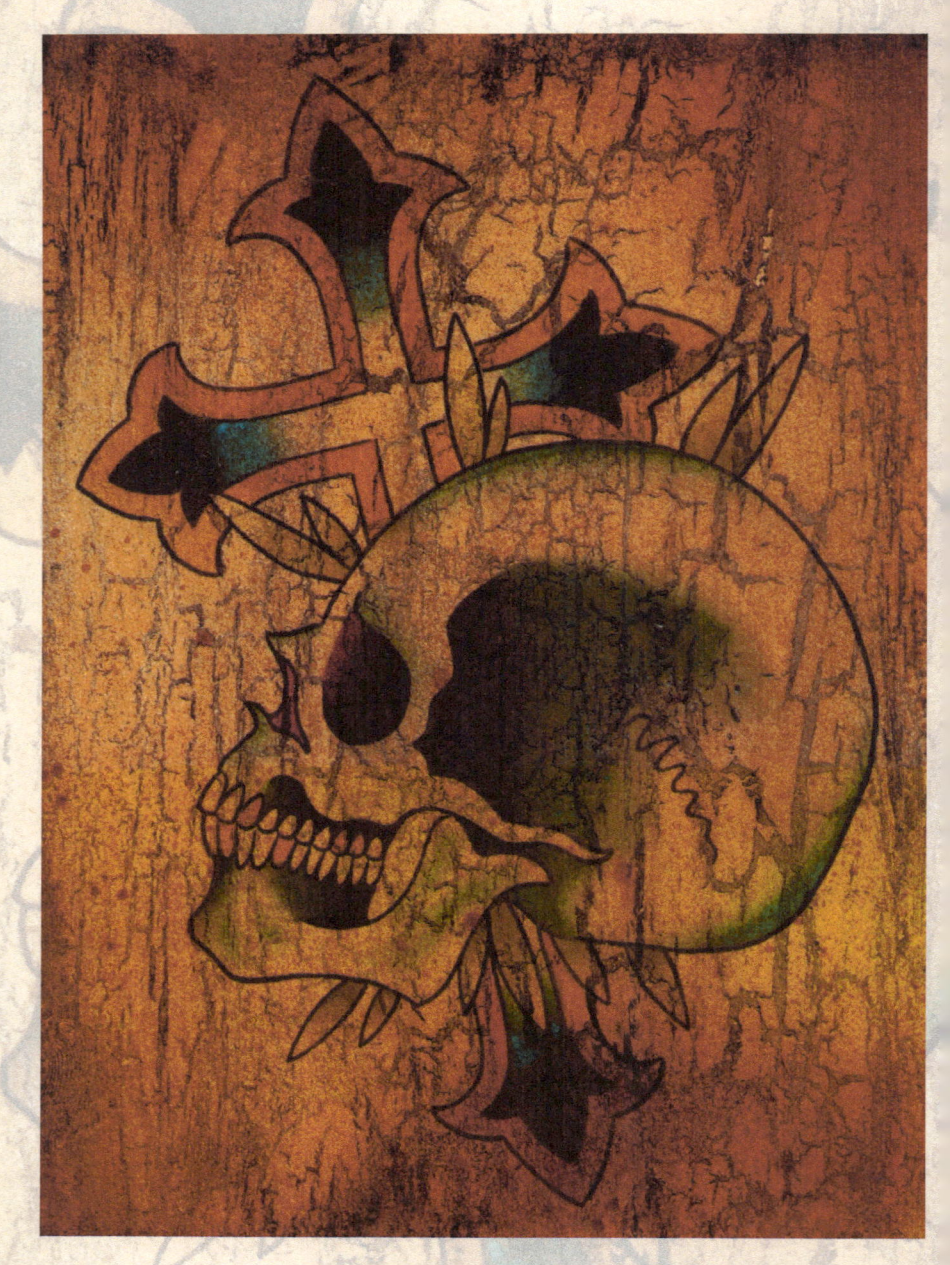

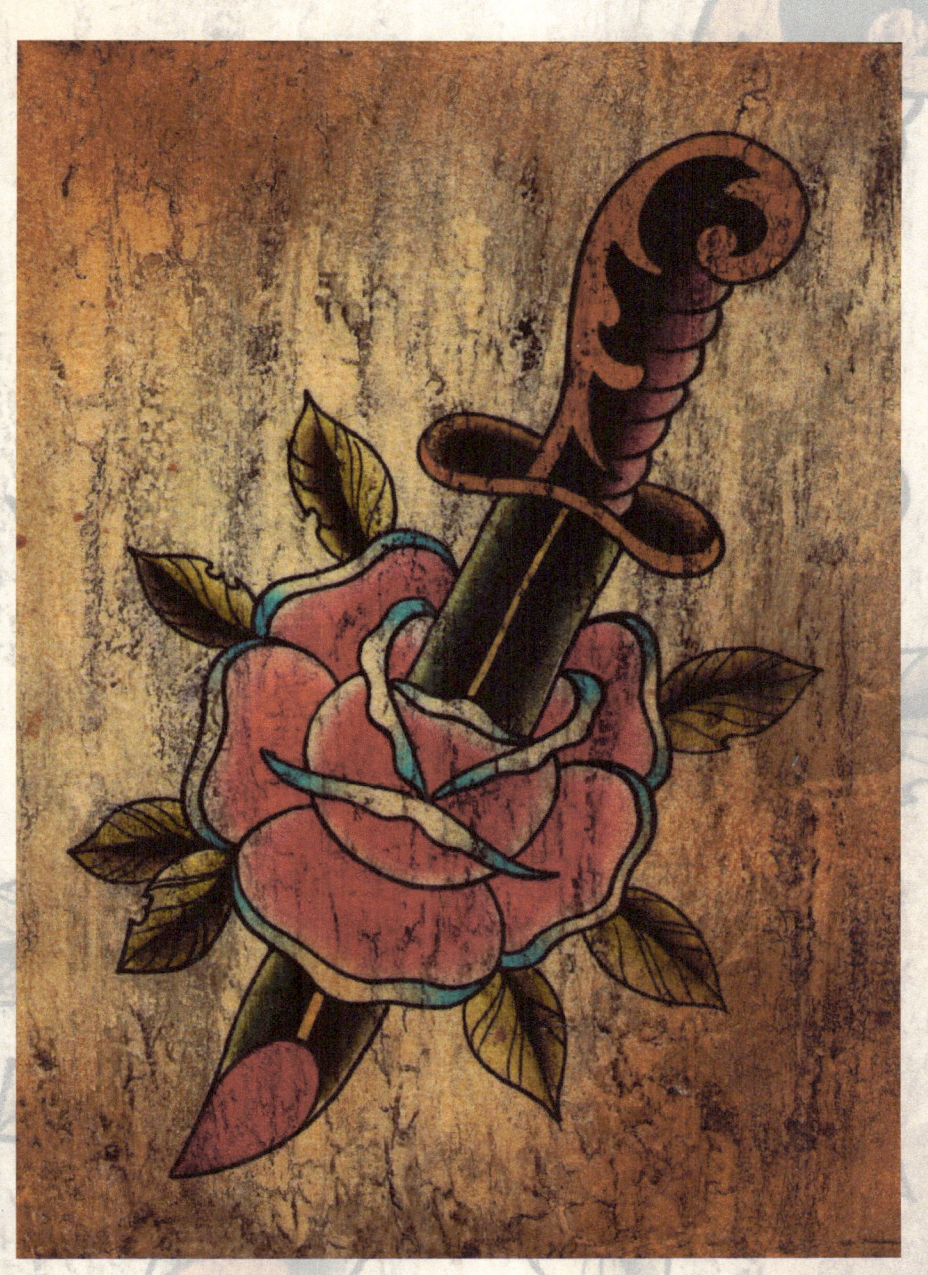

JASON PHILLIPS

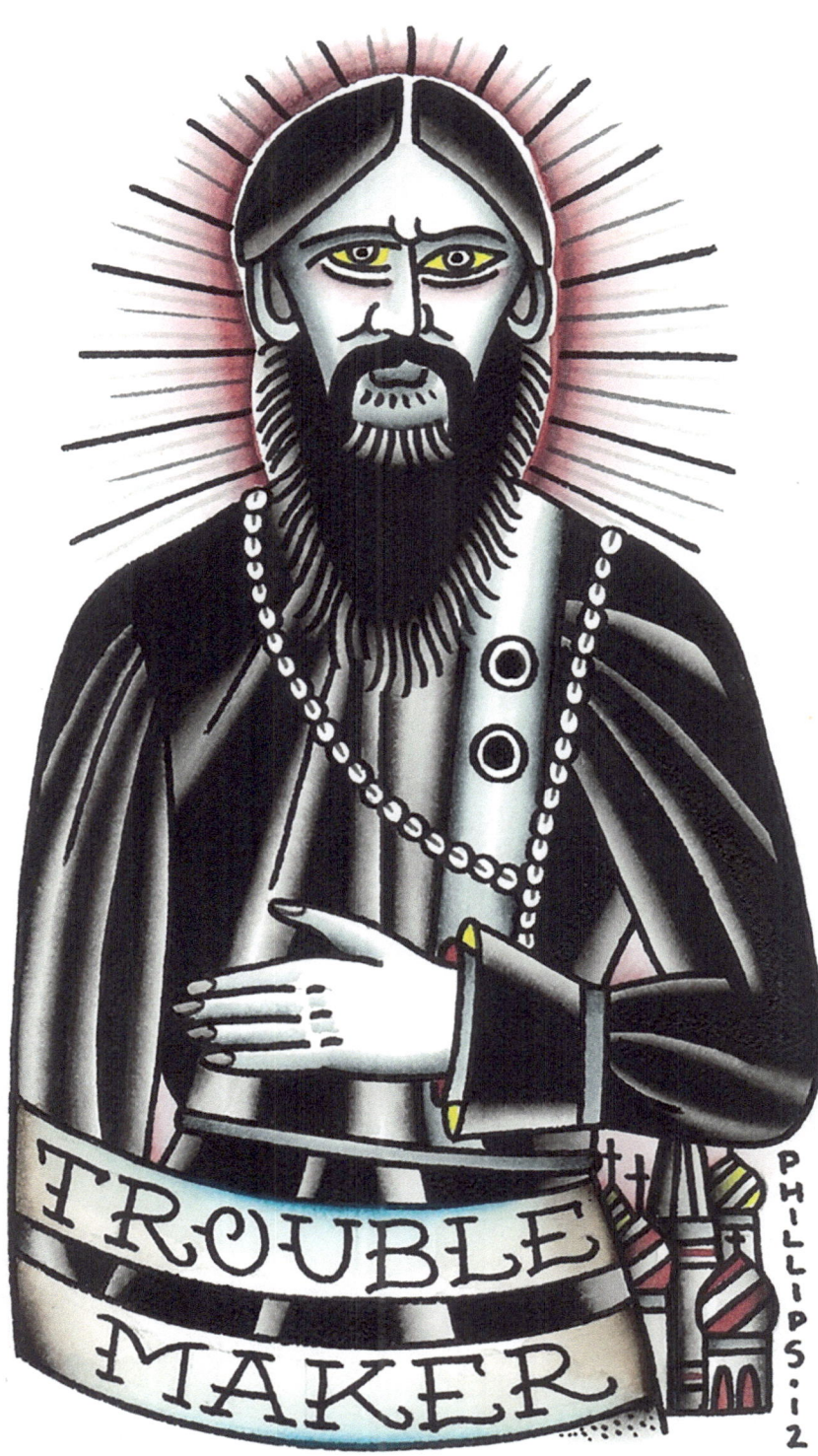

TROUBLE MAKER

PHILLIPS·12

JEF WRIGHT

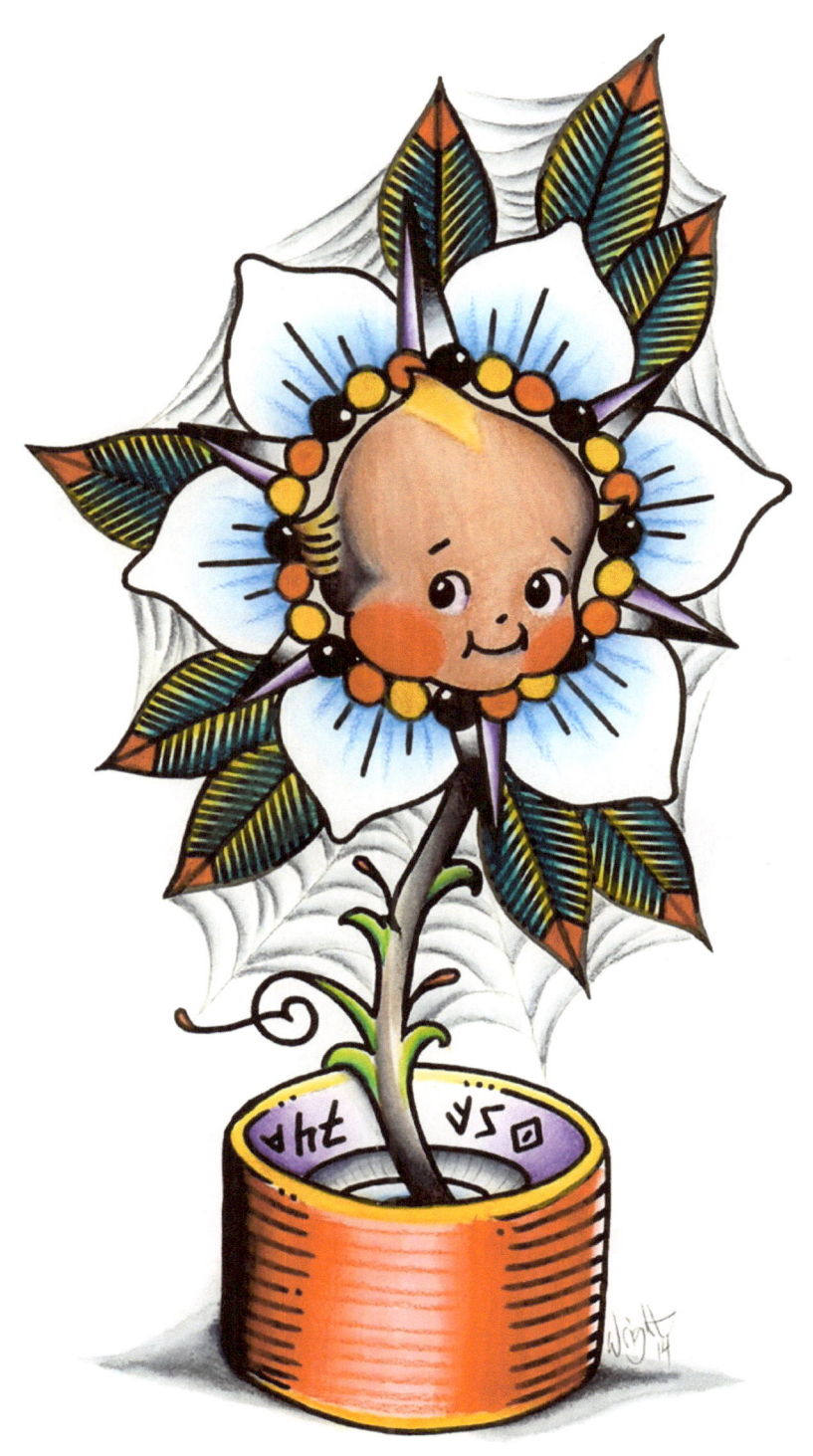

JESSE HANEY

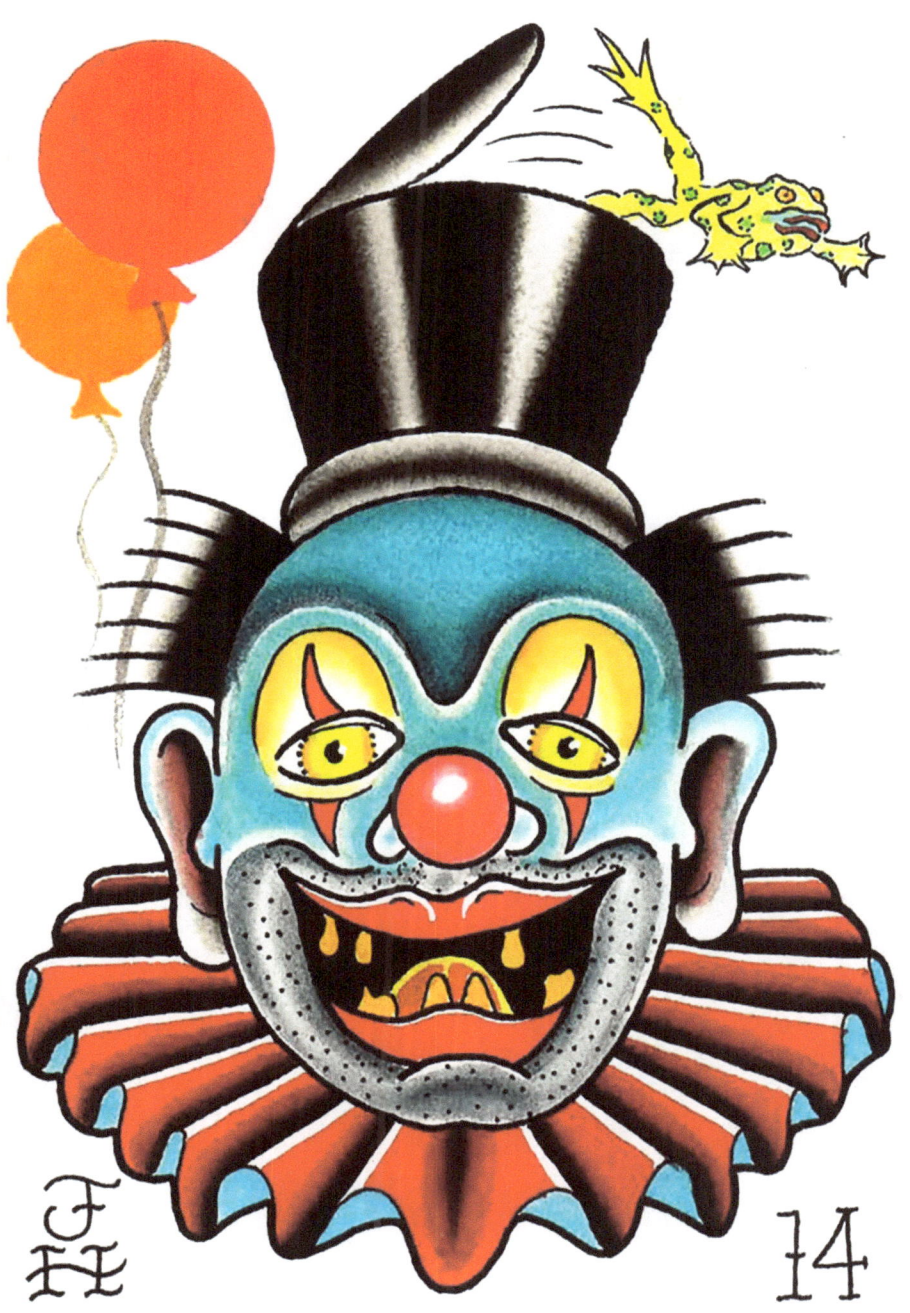

14

40

JESSE SWANSON

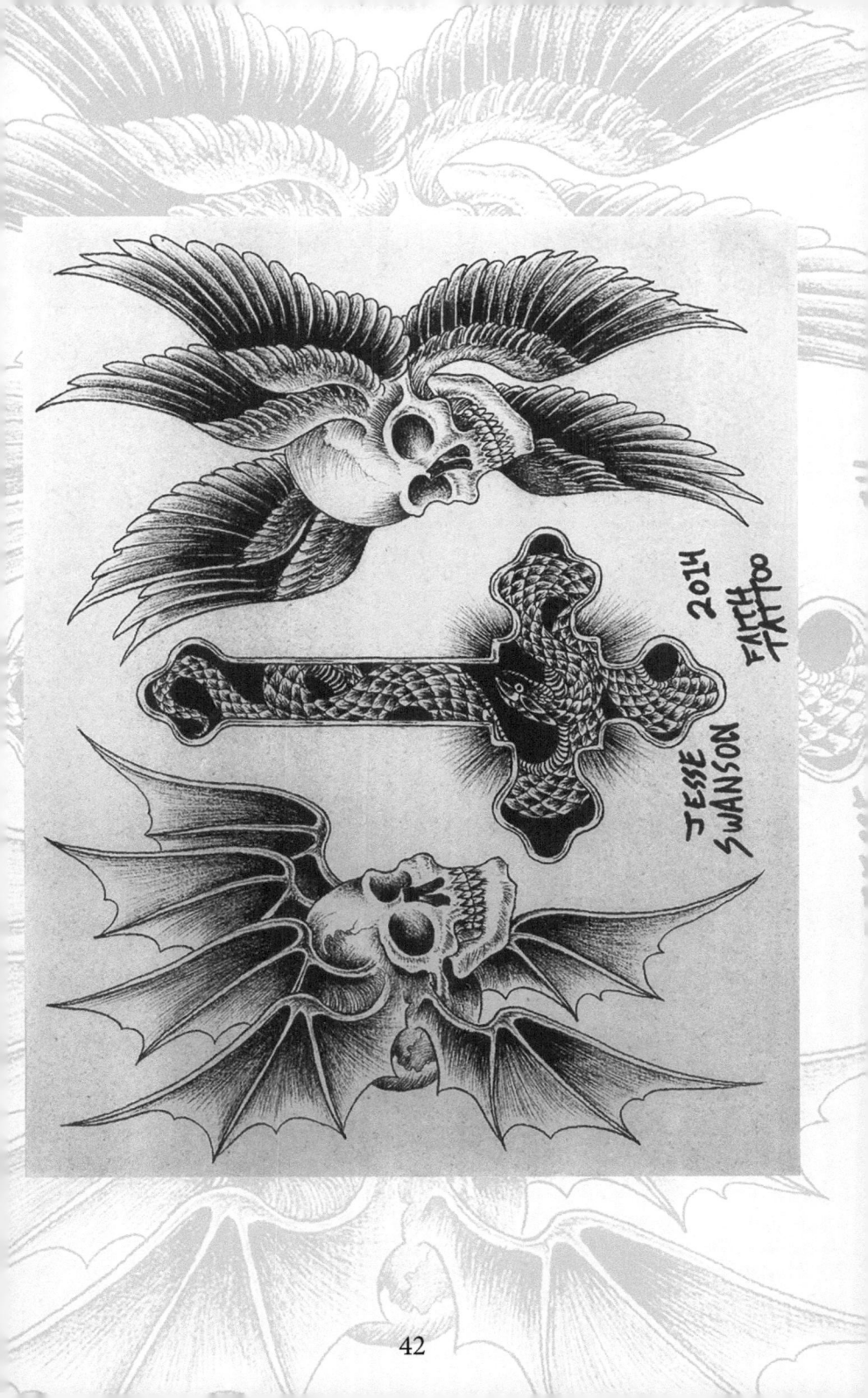

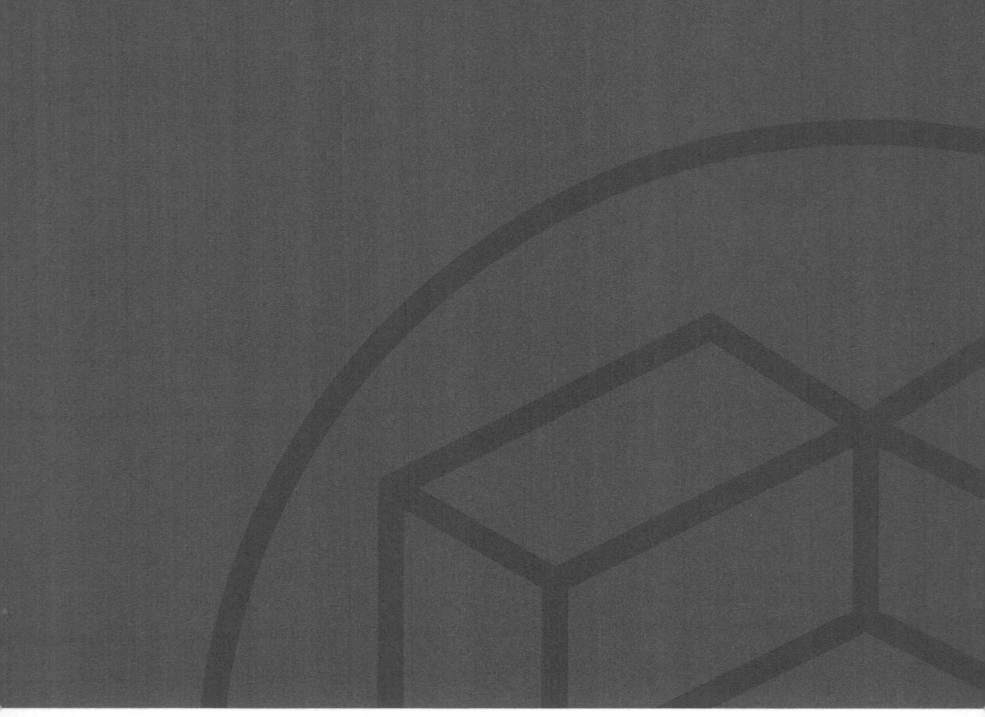

JUSTIN SHAW

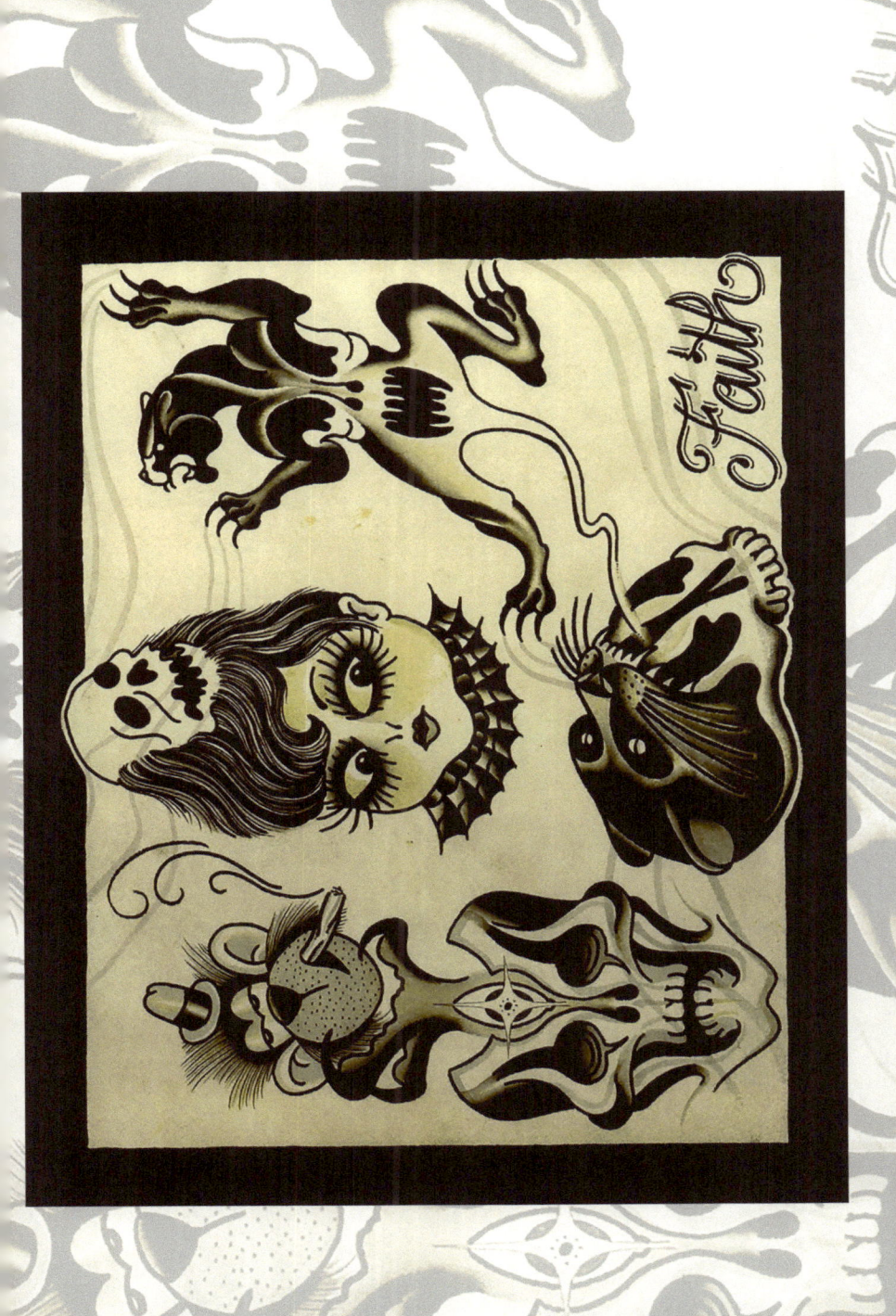

KENNY BROWN

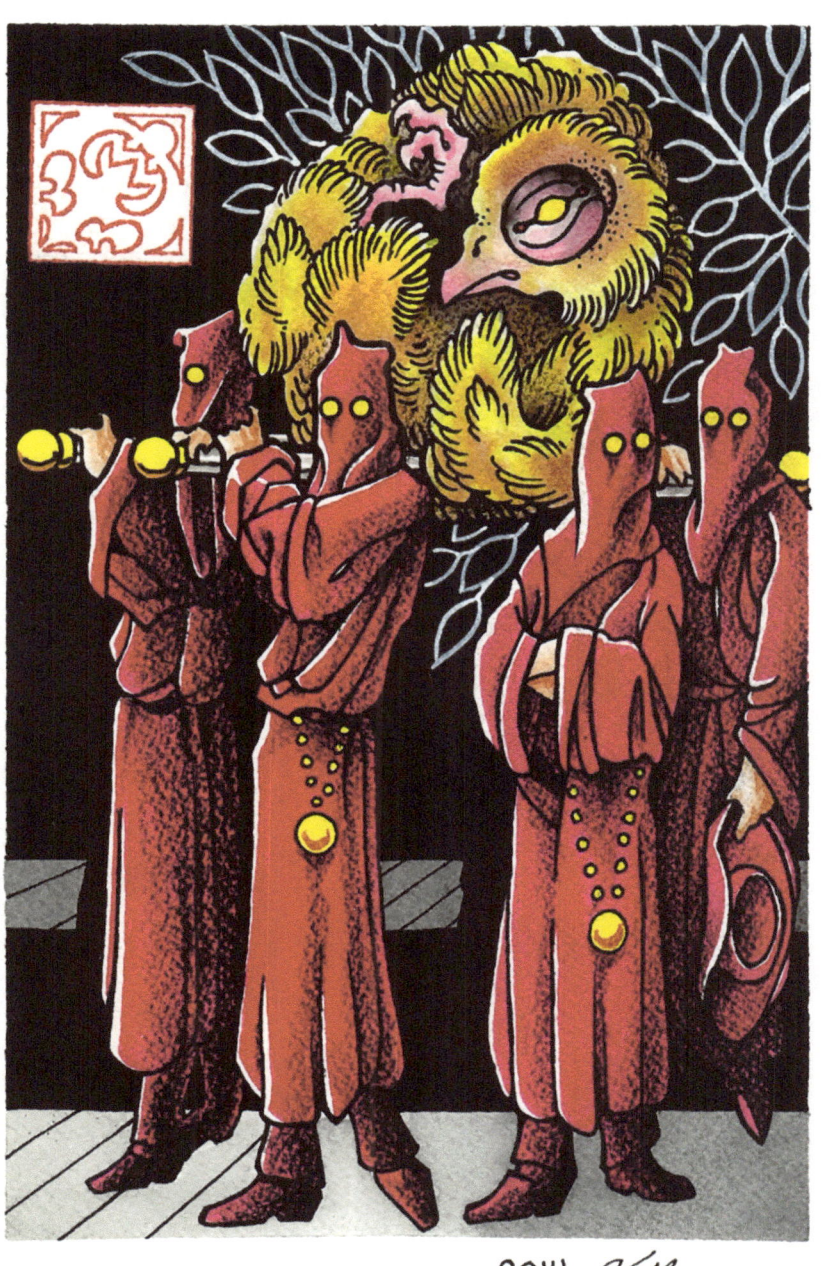

-2014-

NATE GLOMB

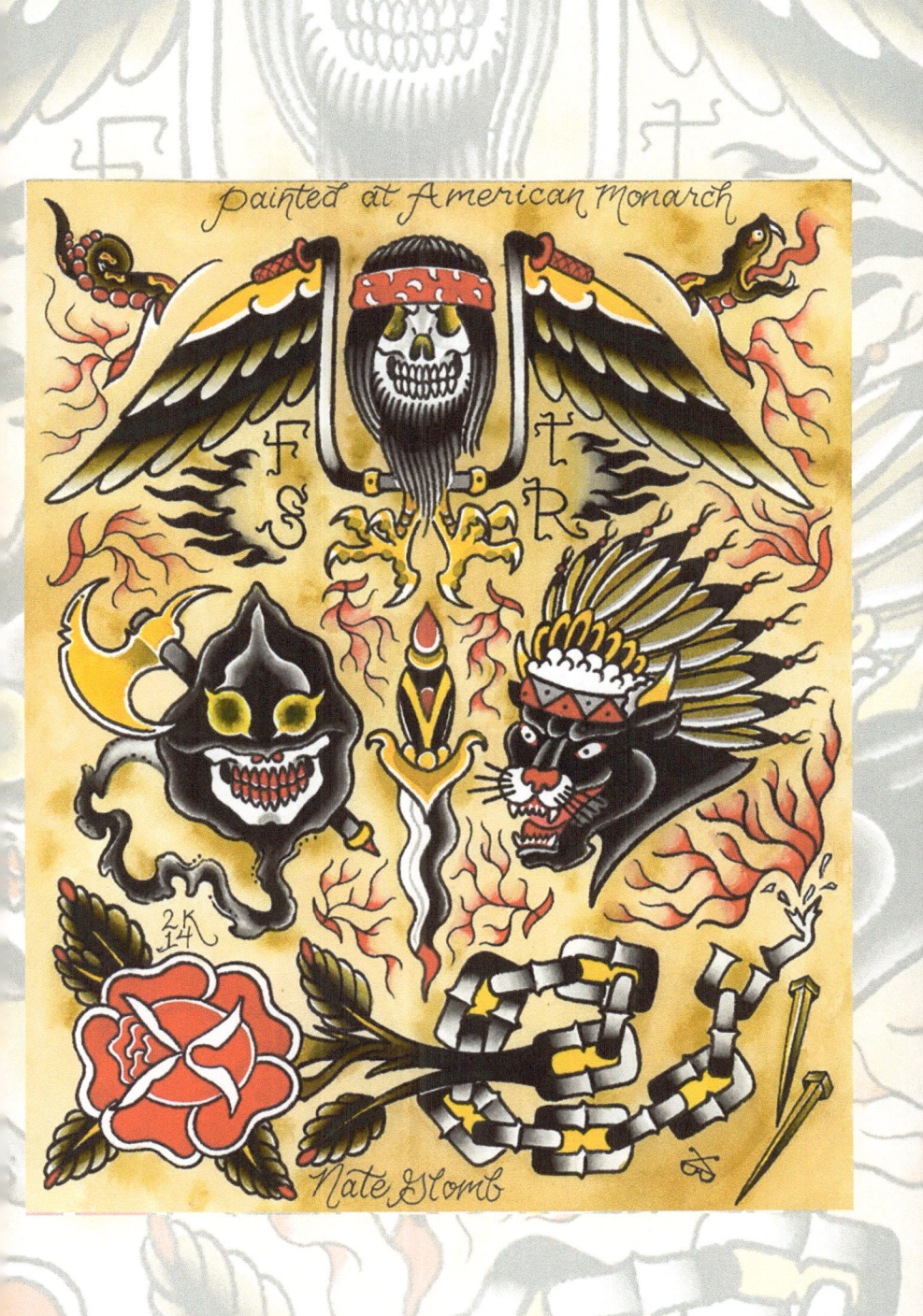

painted at American Monarch

Nate Slomb

NICK PAINE

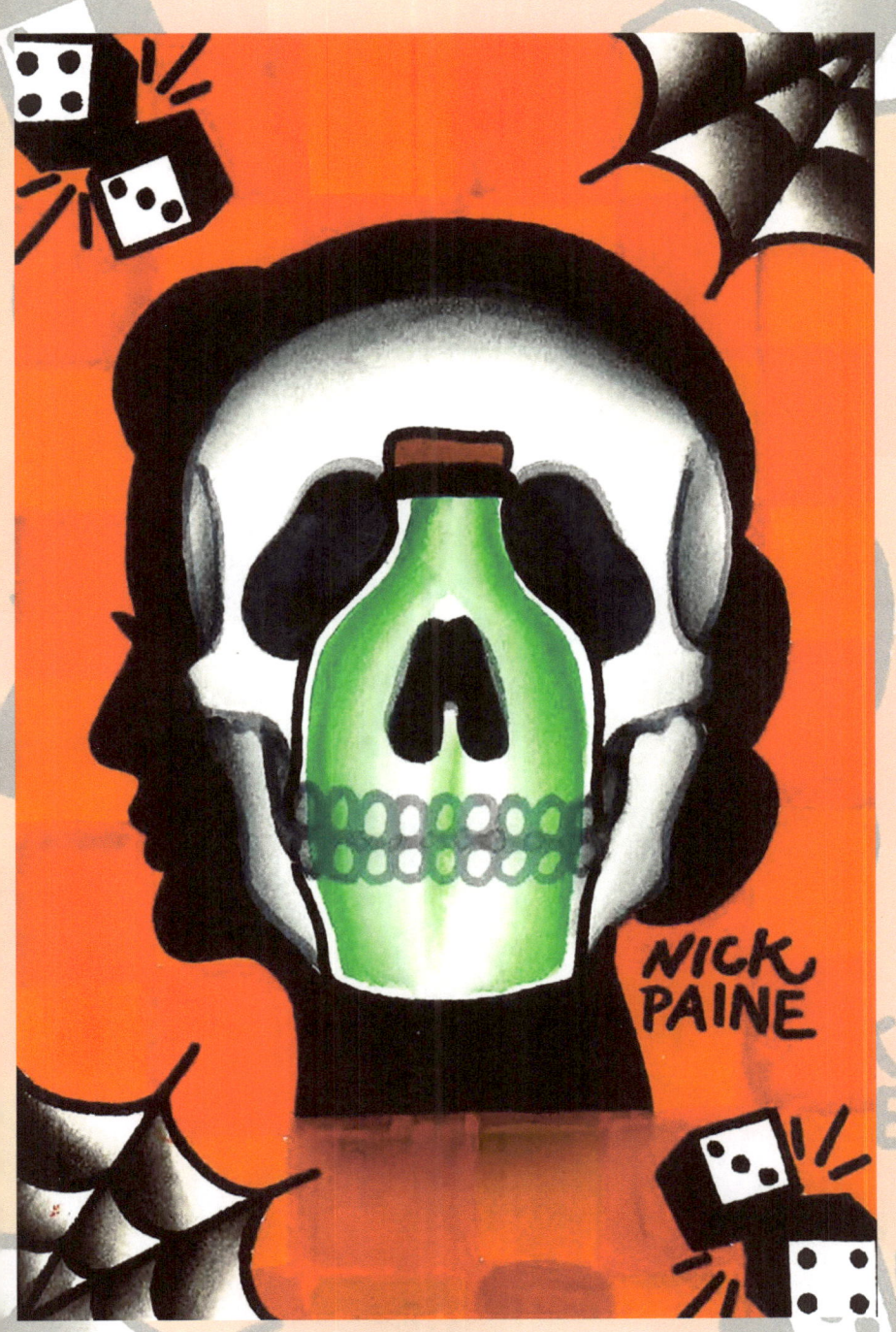

50

RJ HITCHCOCK

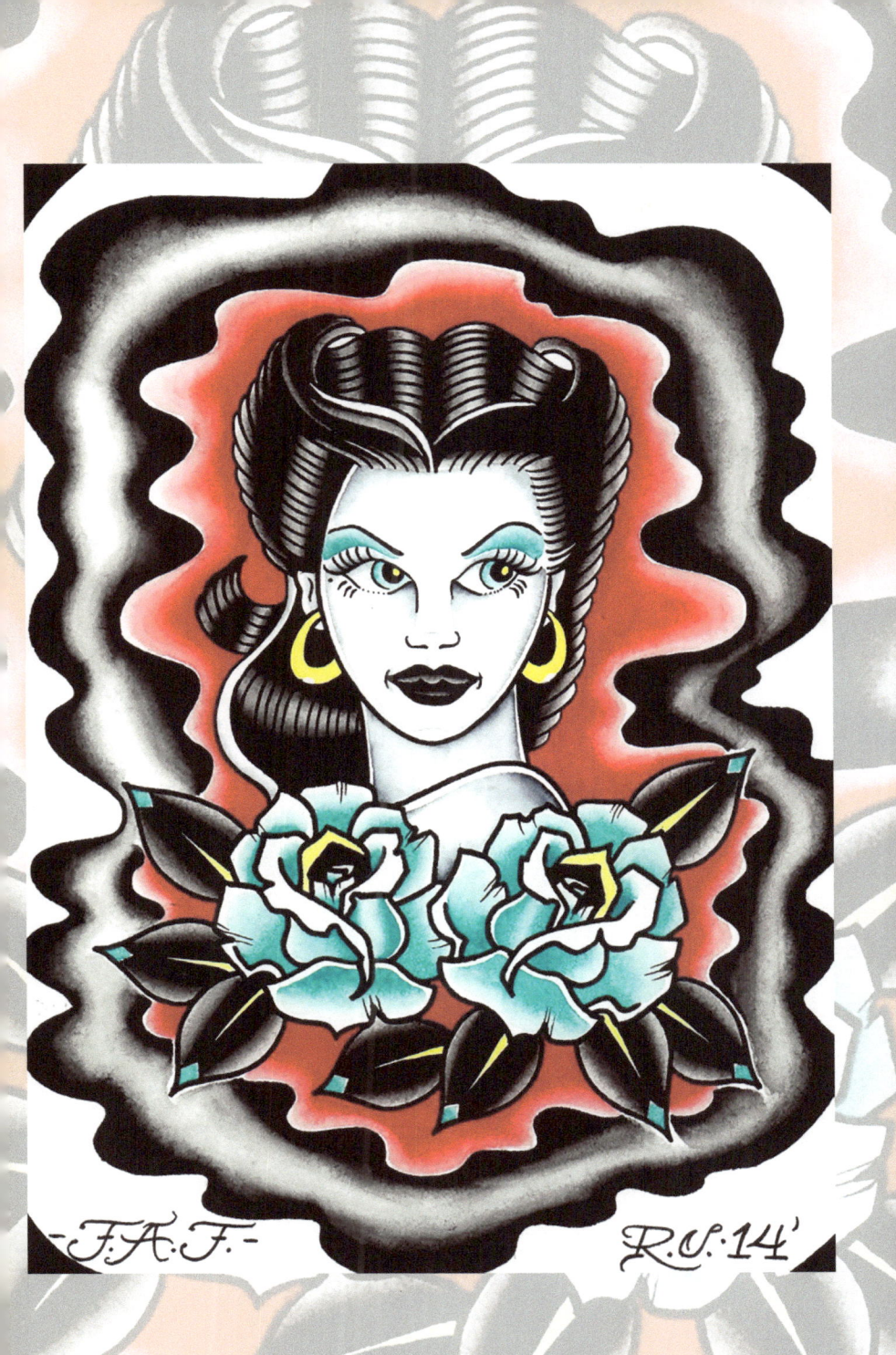

RYAN TANTON

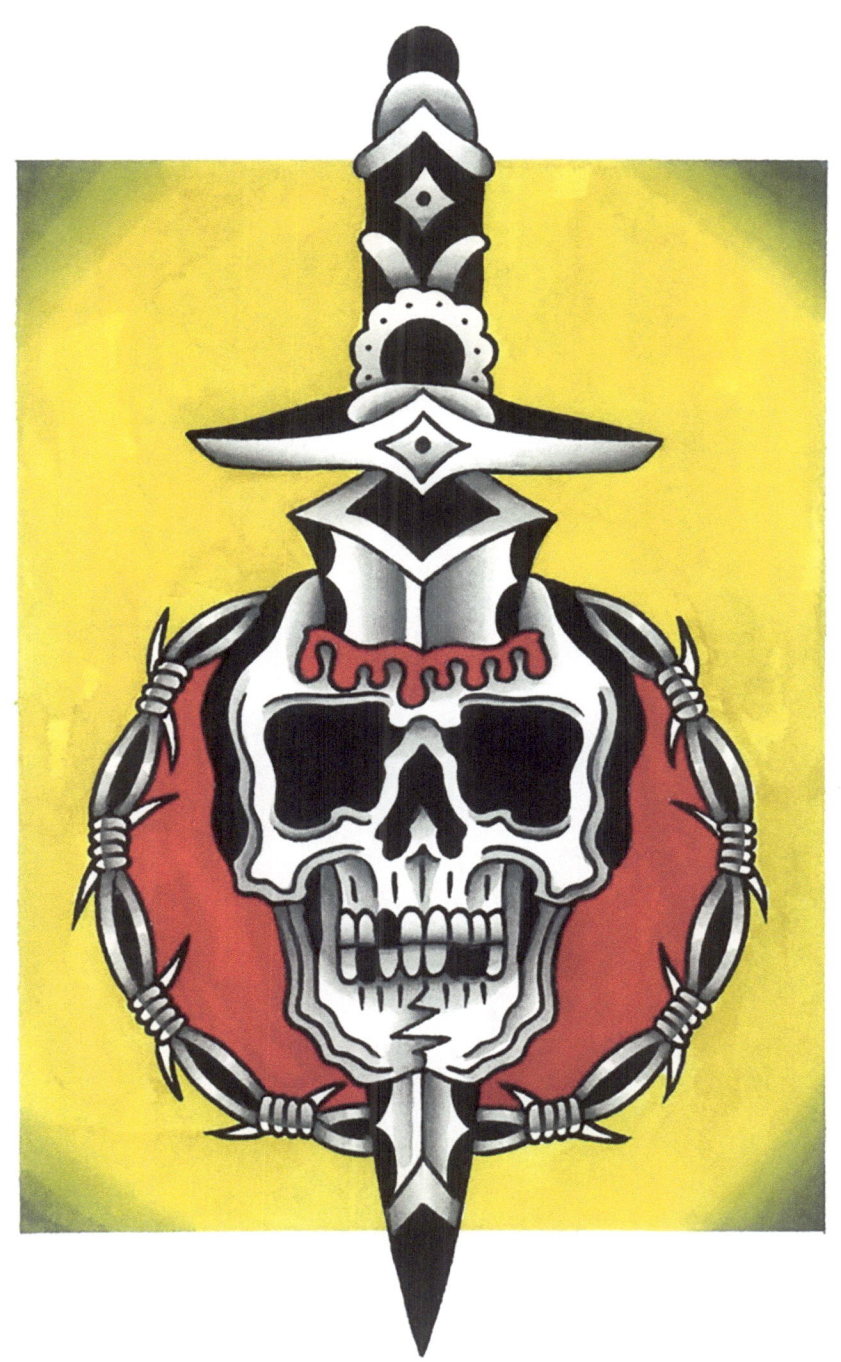

TANTON 2014

SEAN PERKINSON

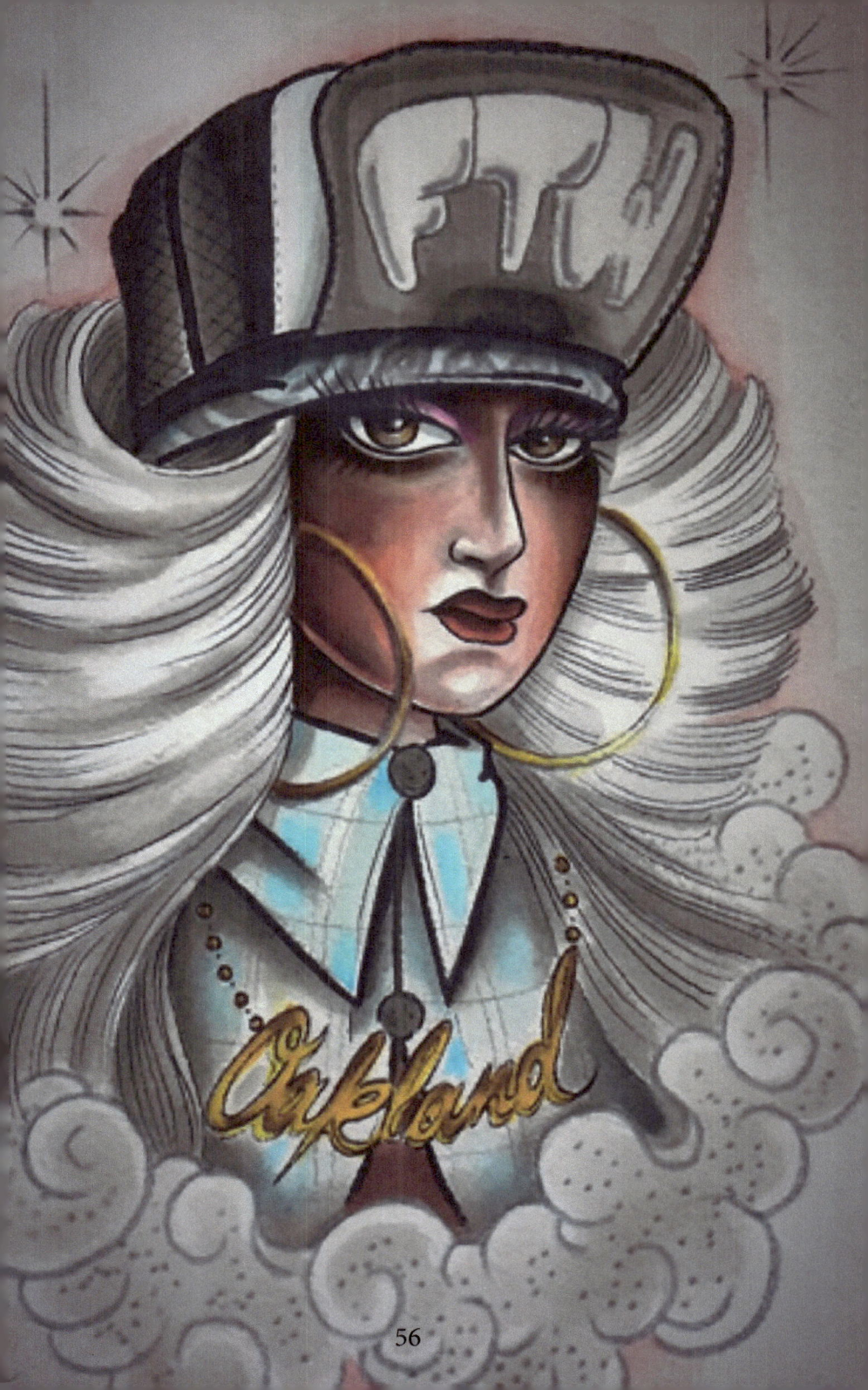

STEVE RIECK

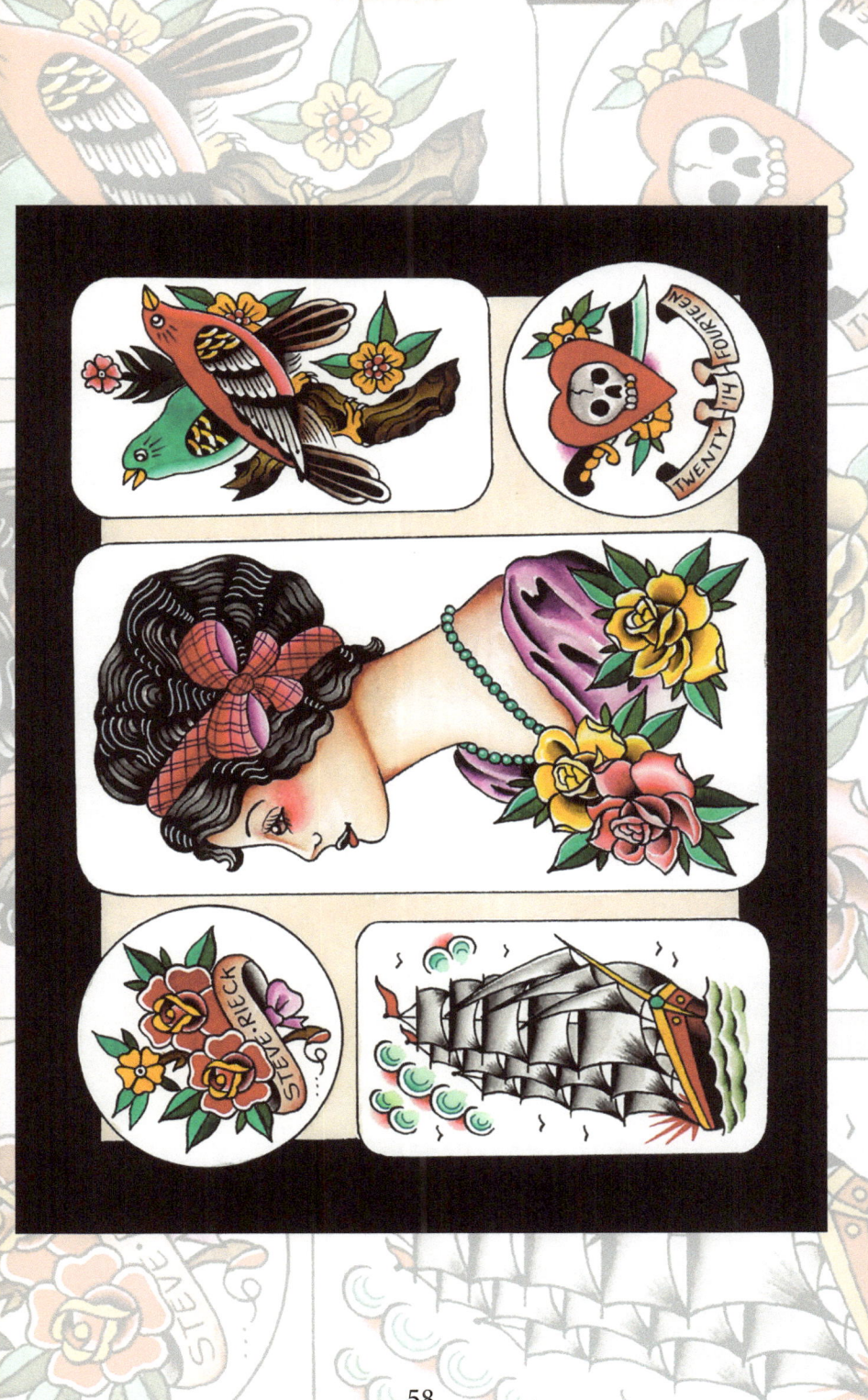

TYLER LUNT

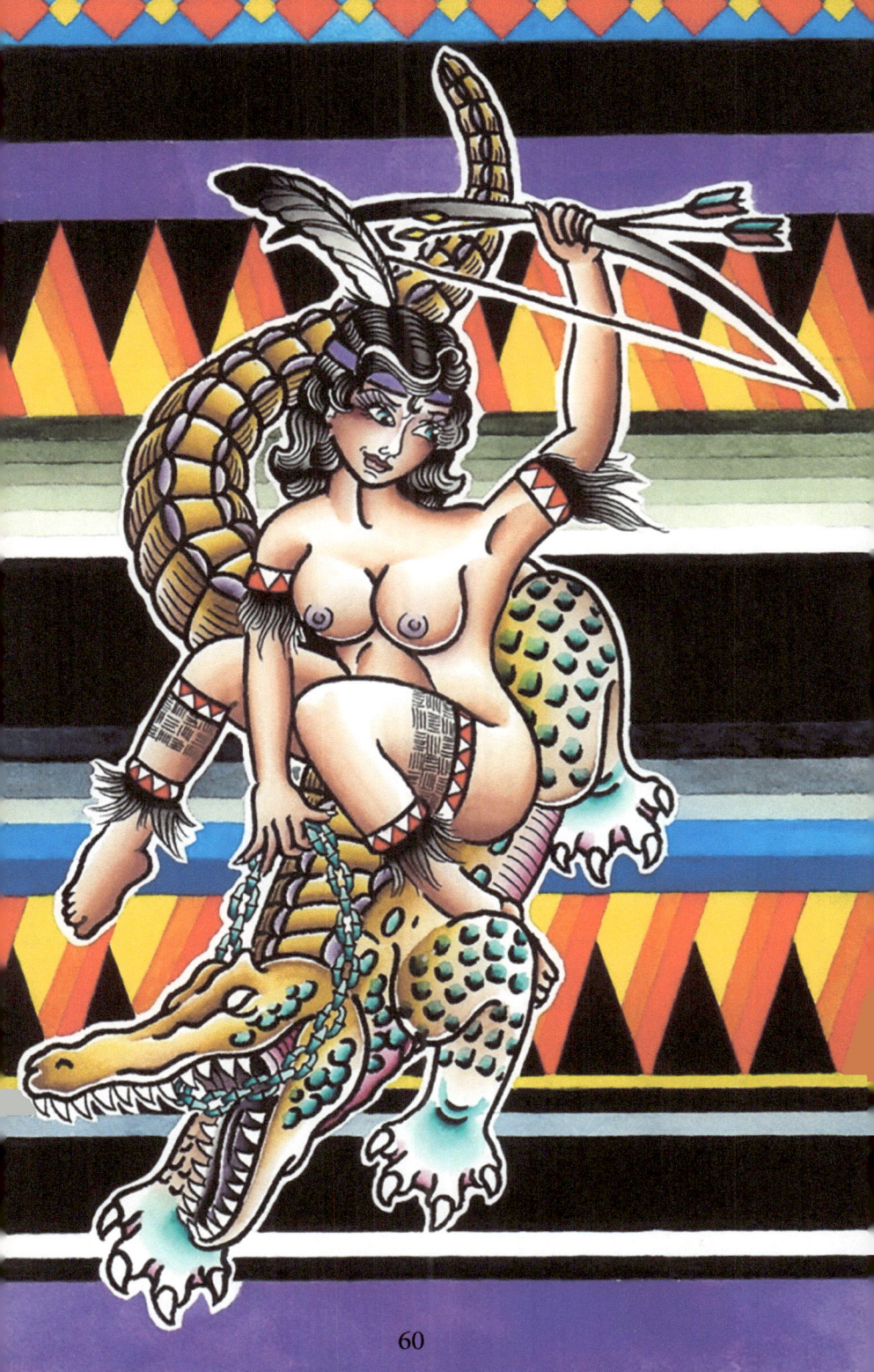

60

WALTER MCDONALD

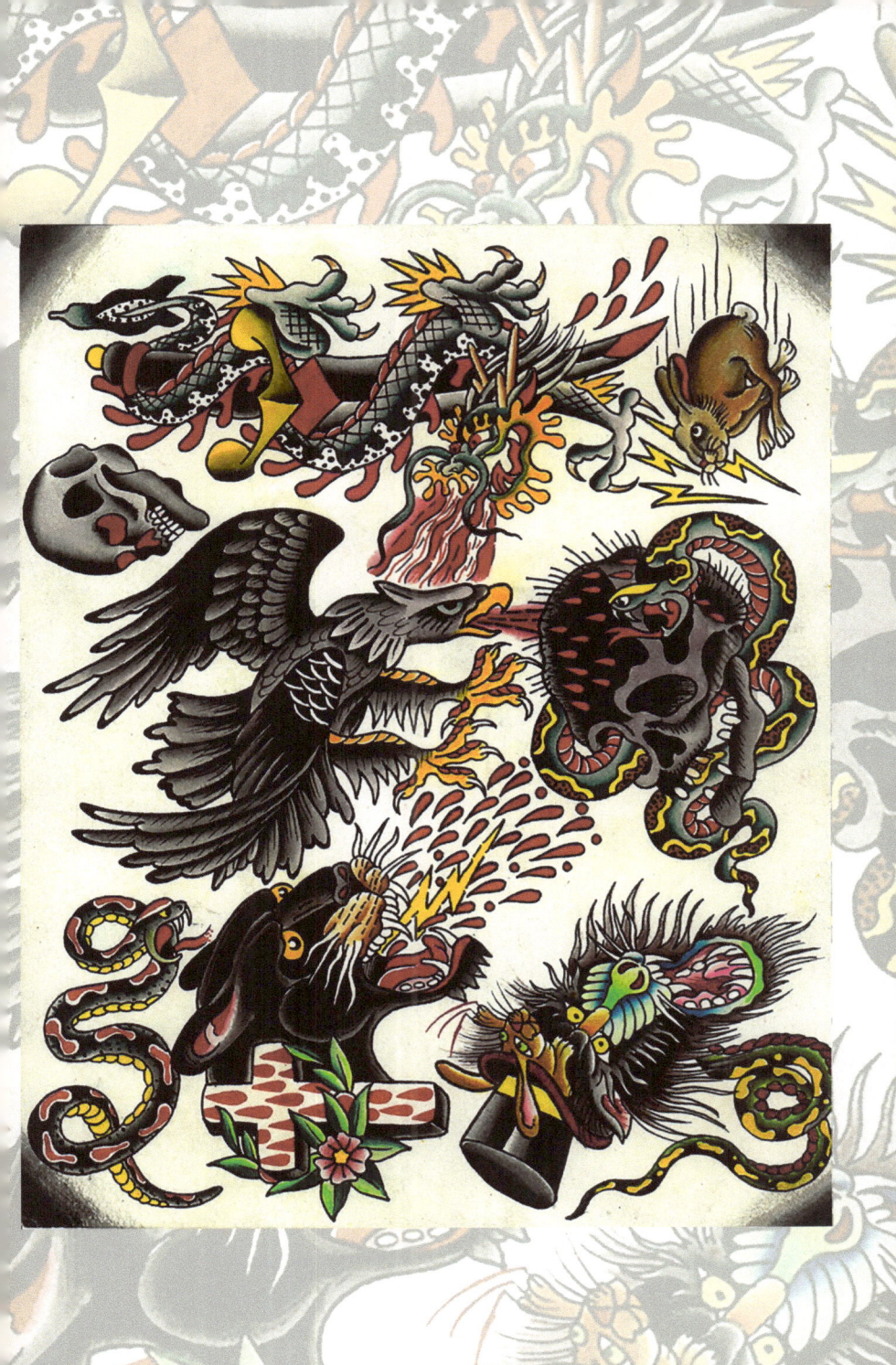

WALTER McDONALD

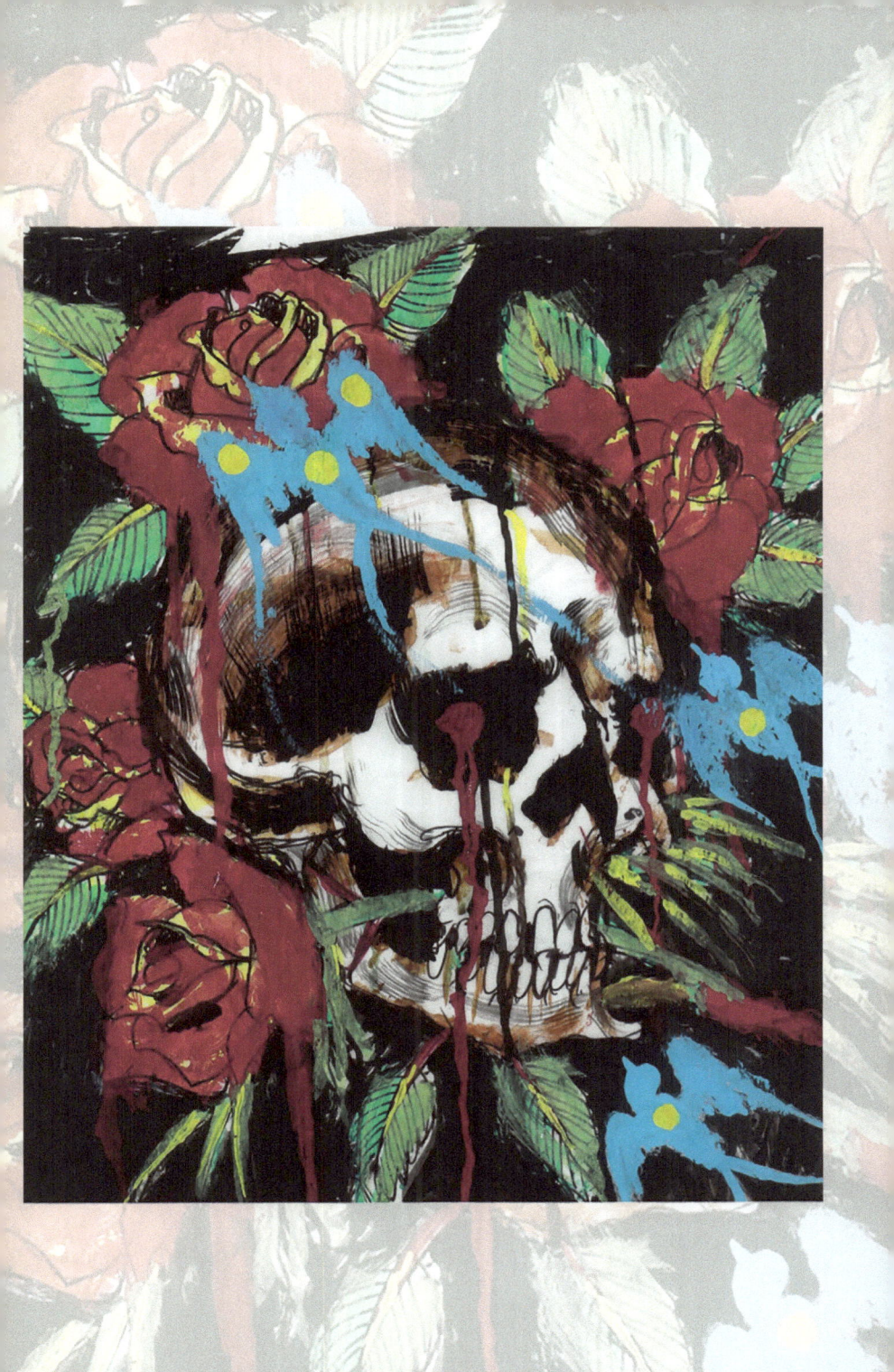

WESLEY JACKSON

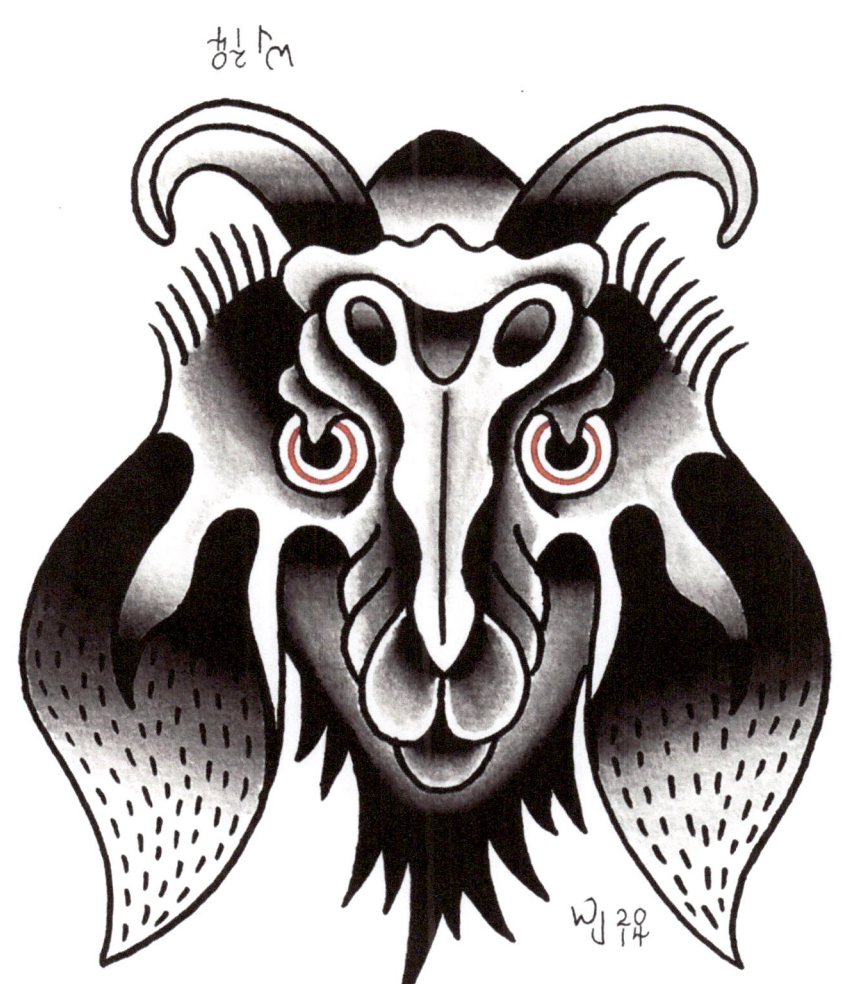

WRATH

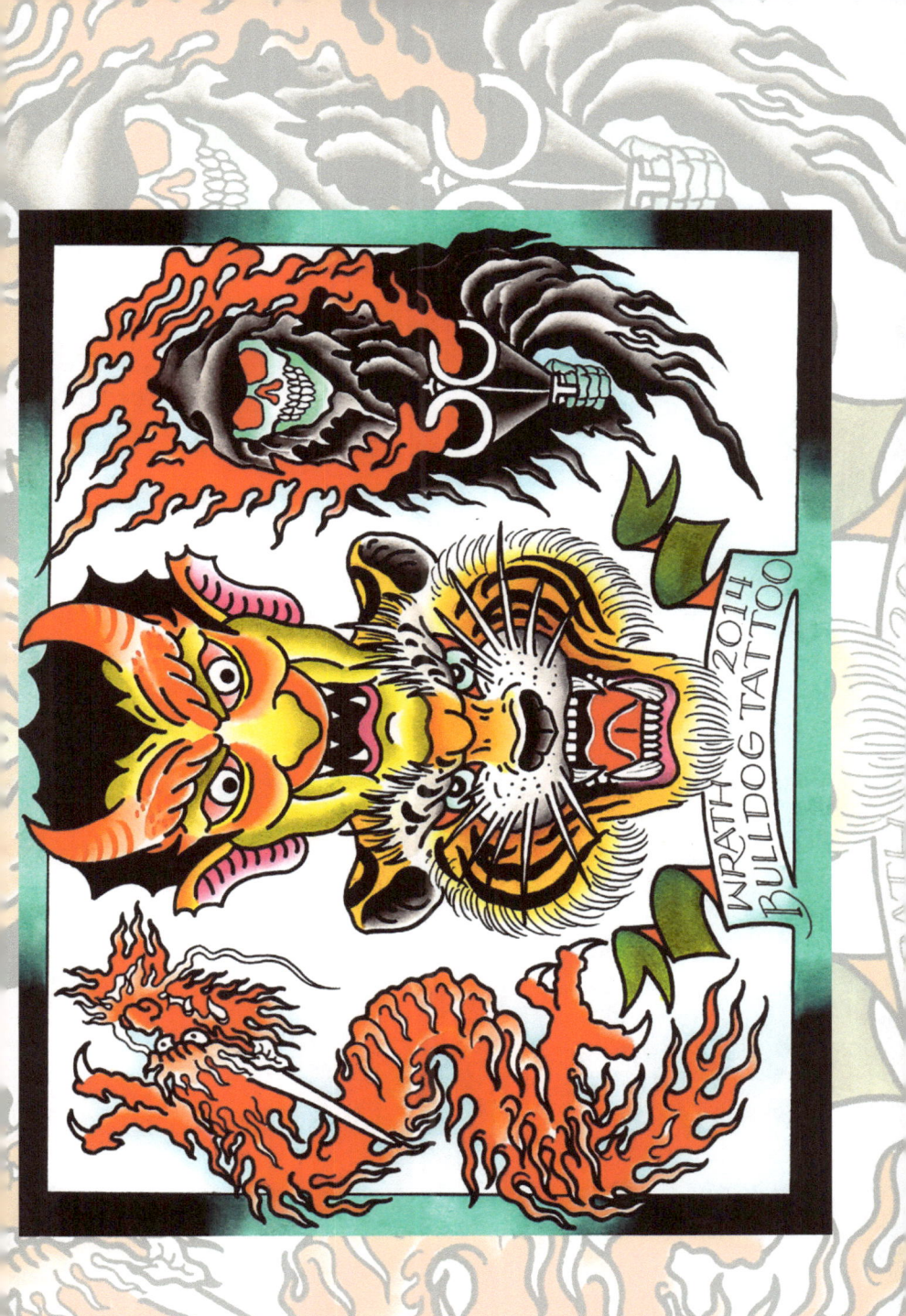

FREEMAN & SHAW

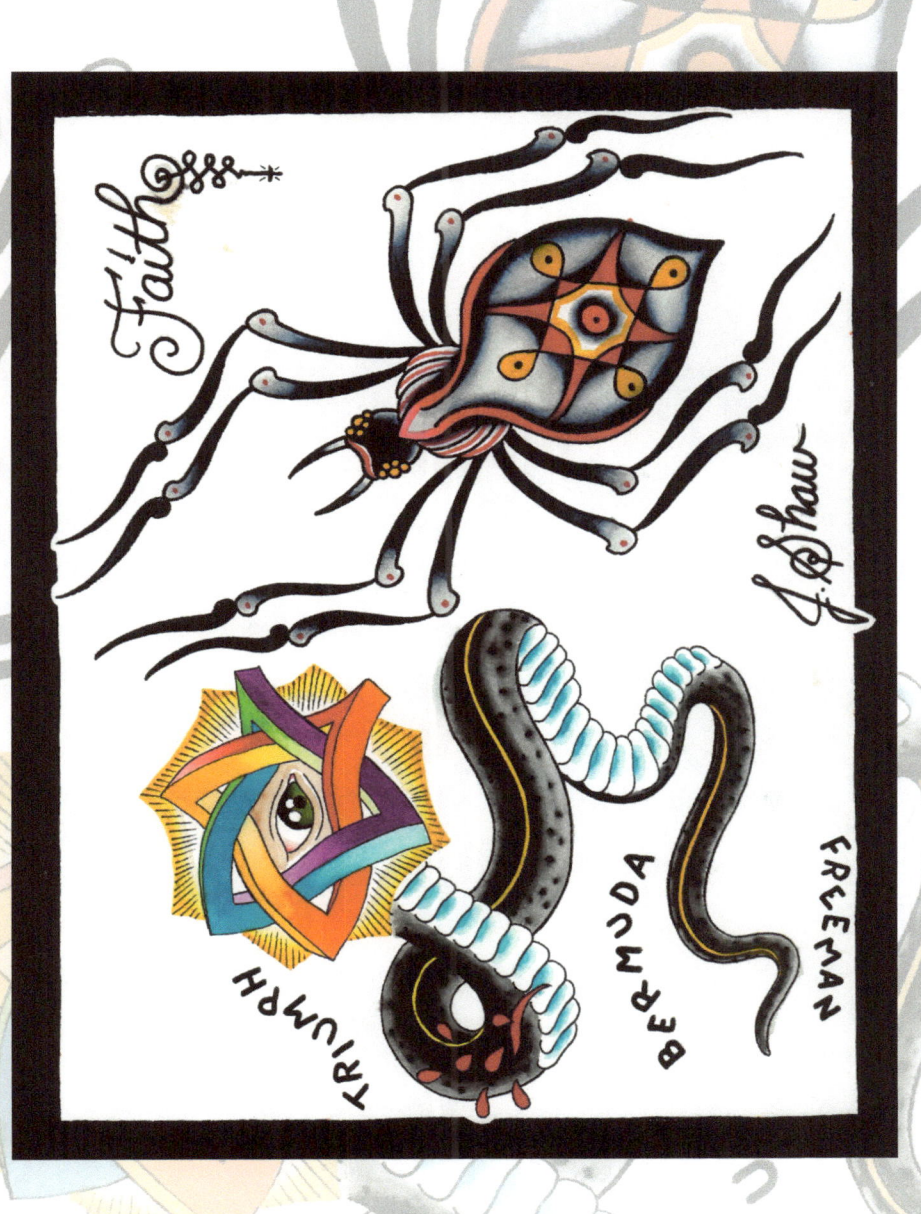

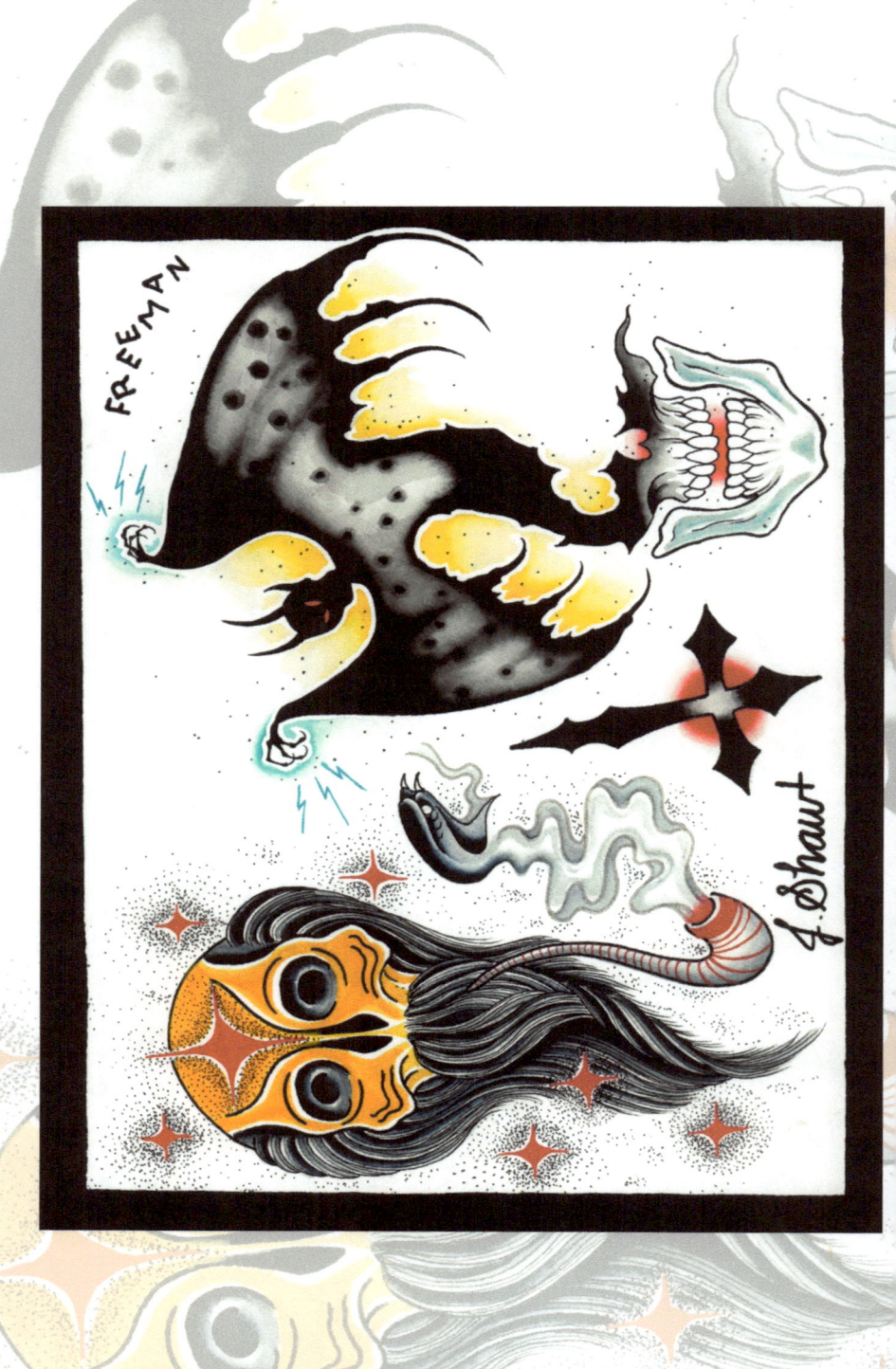

71

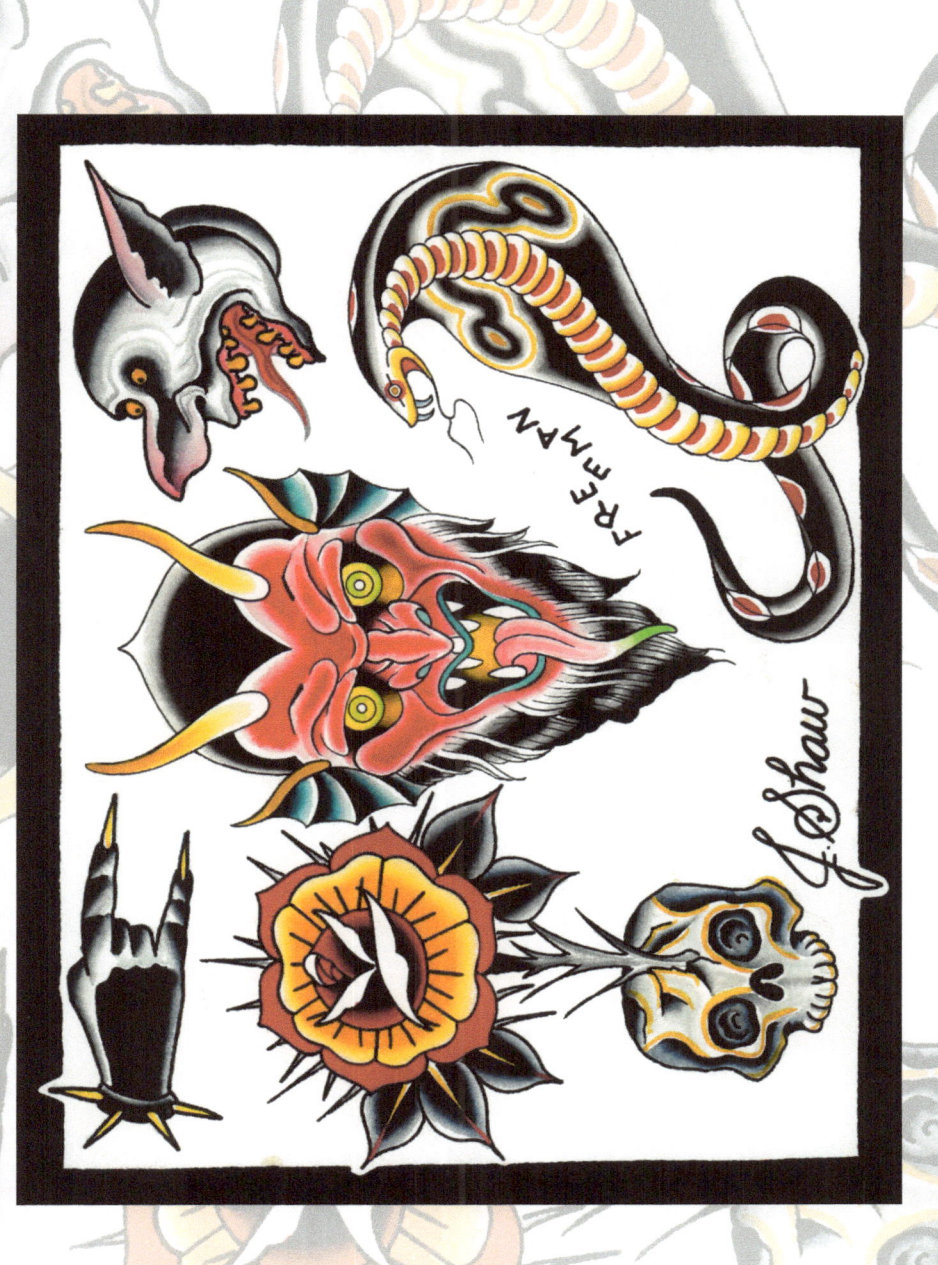

FREEMAN

J. Shaw

LEE HANNA

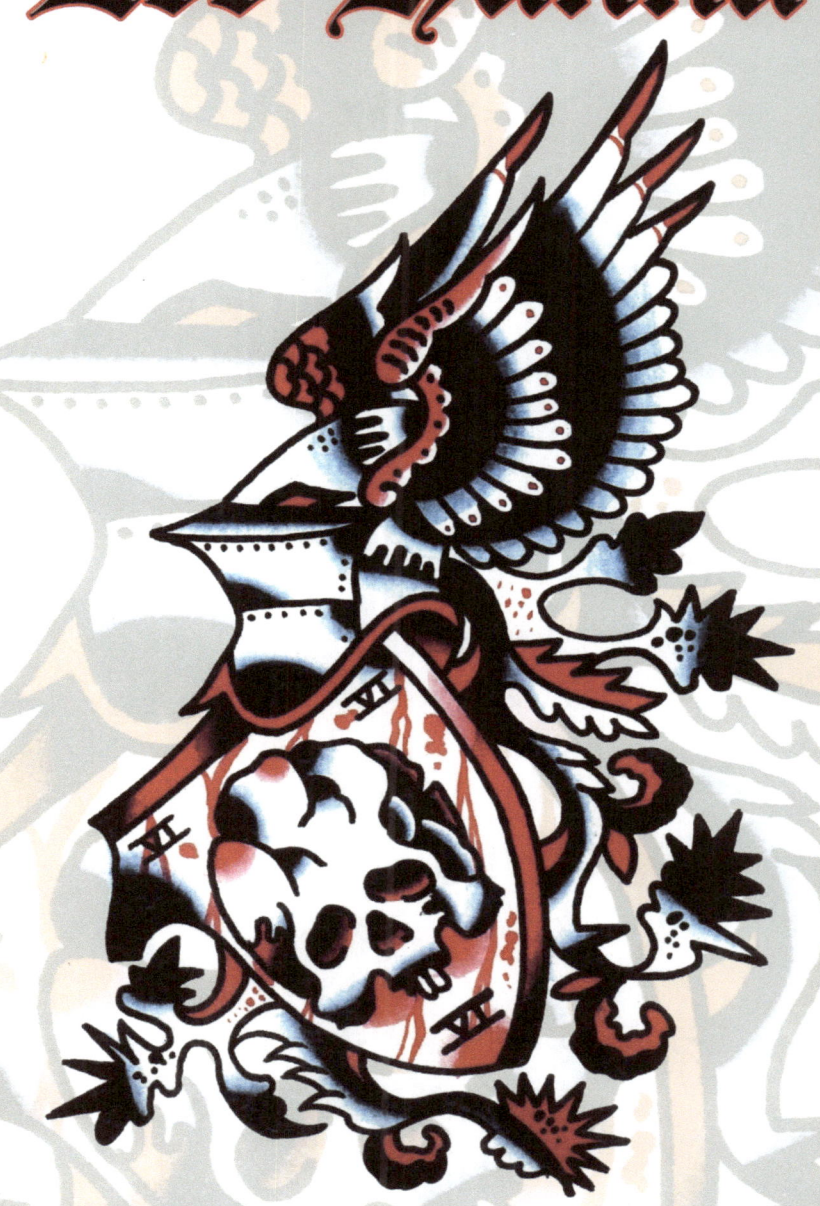

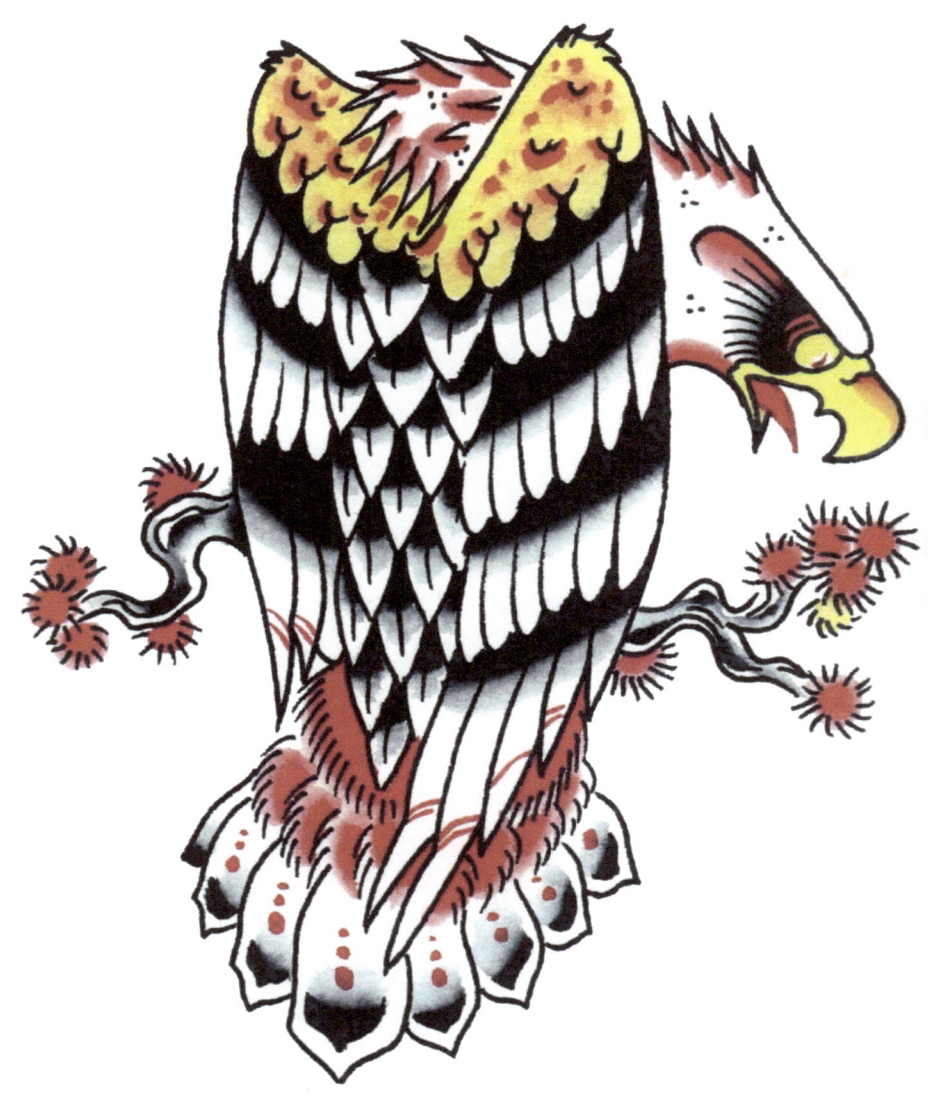

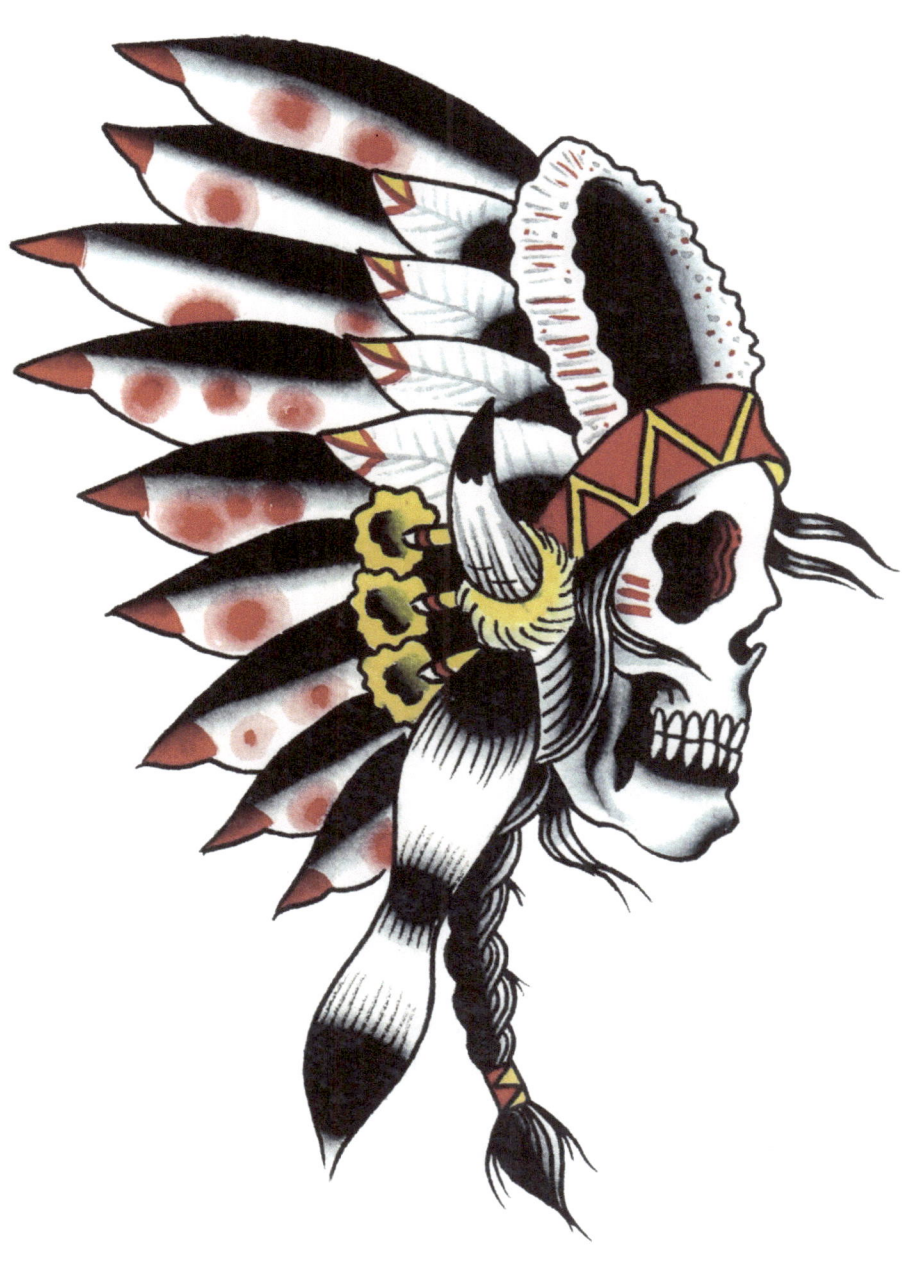

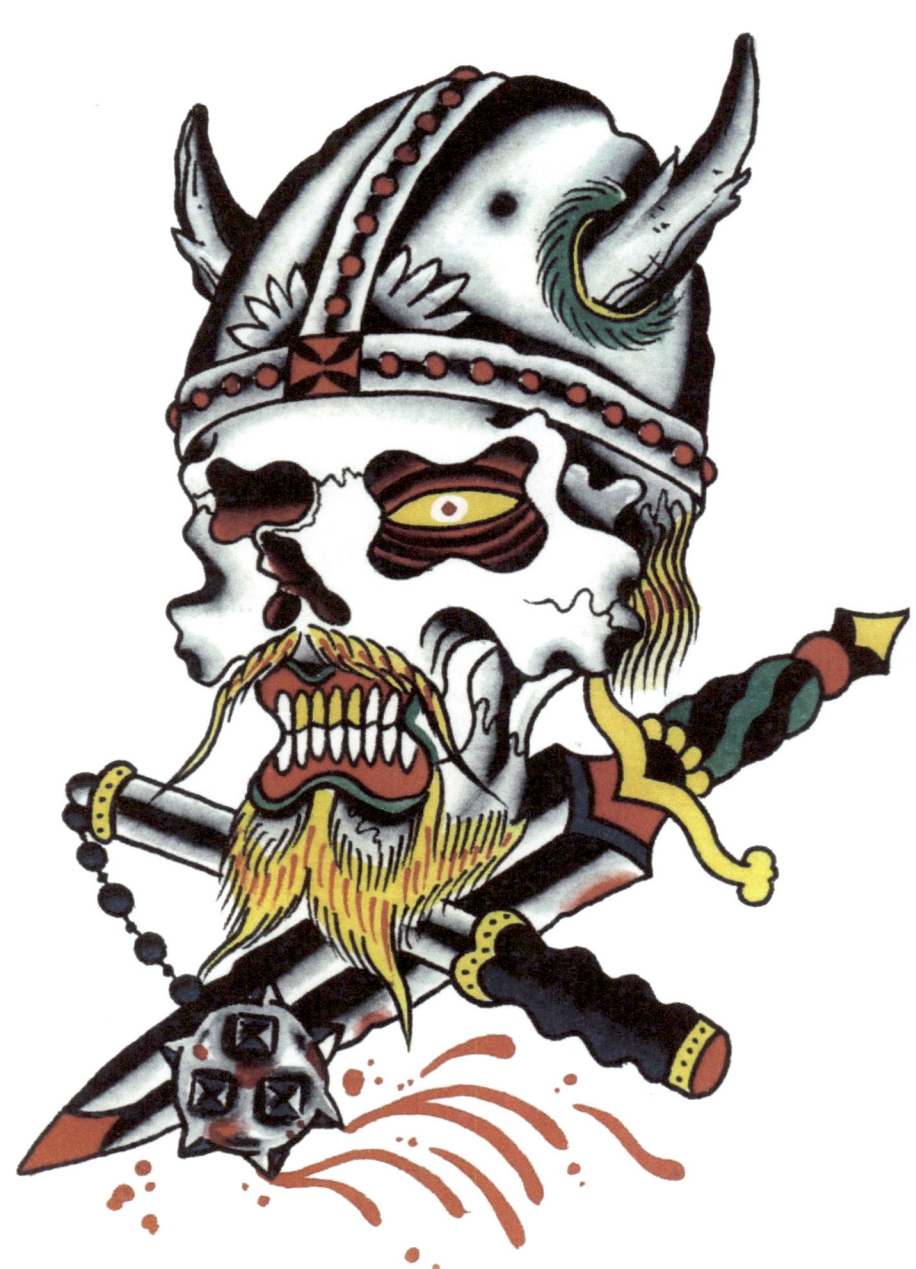

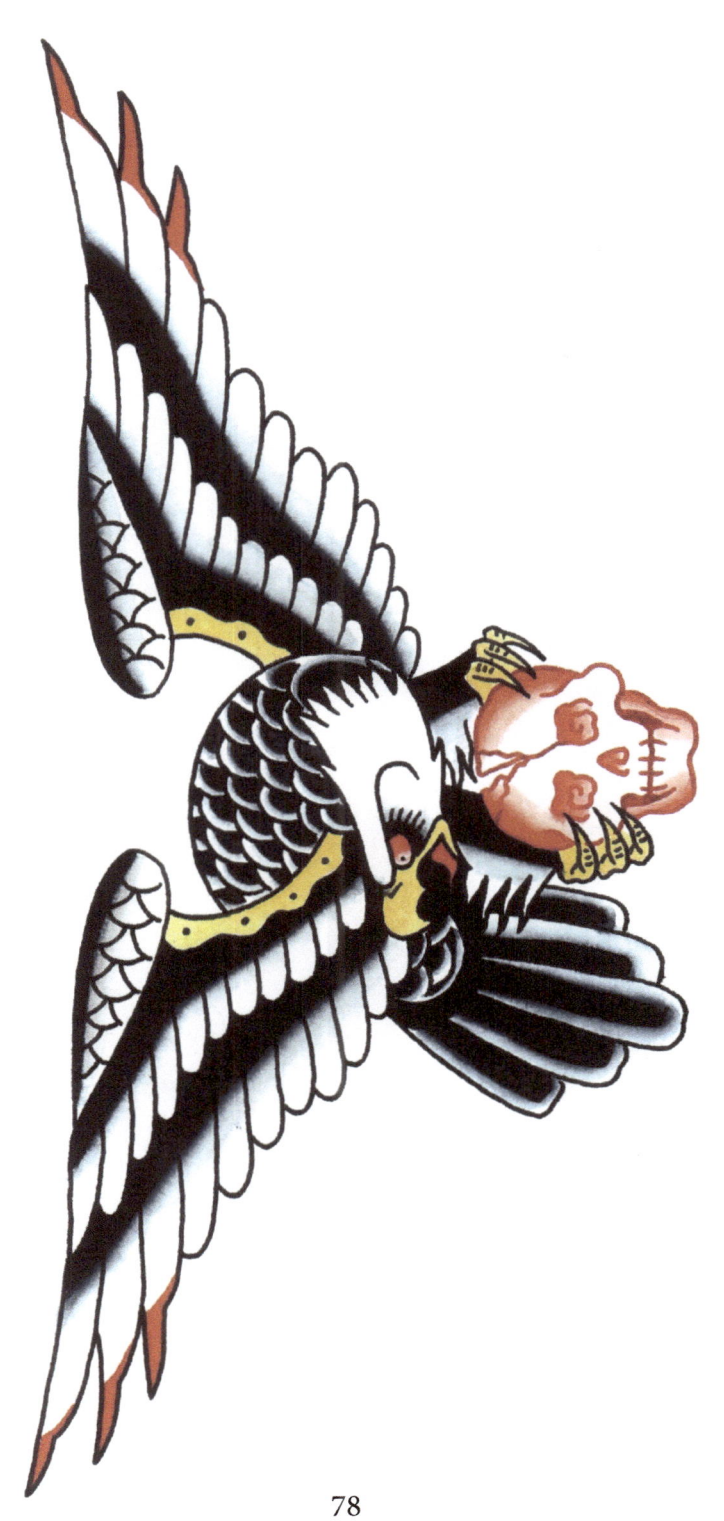

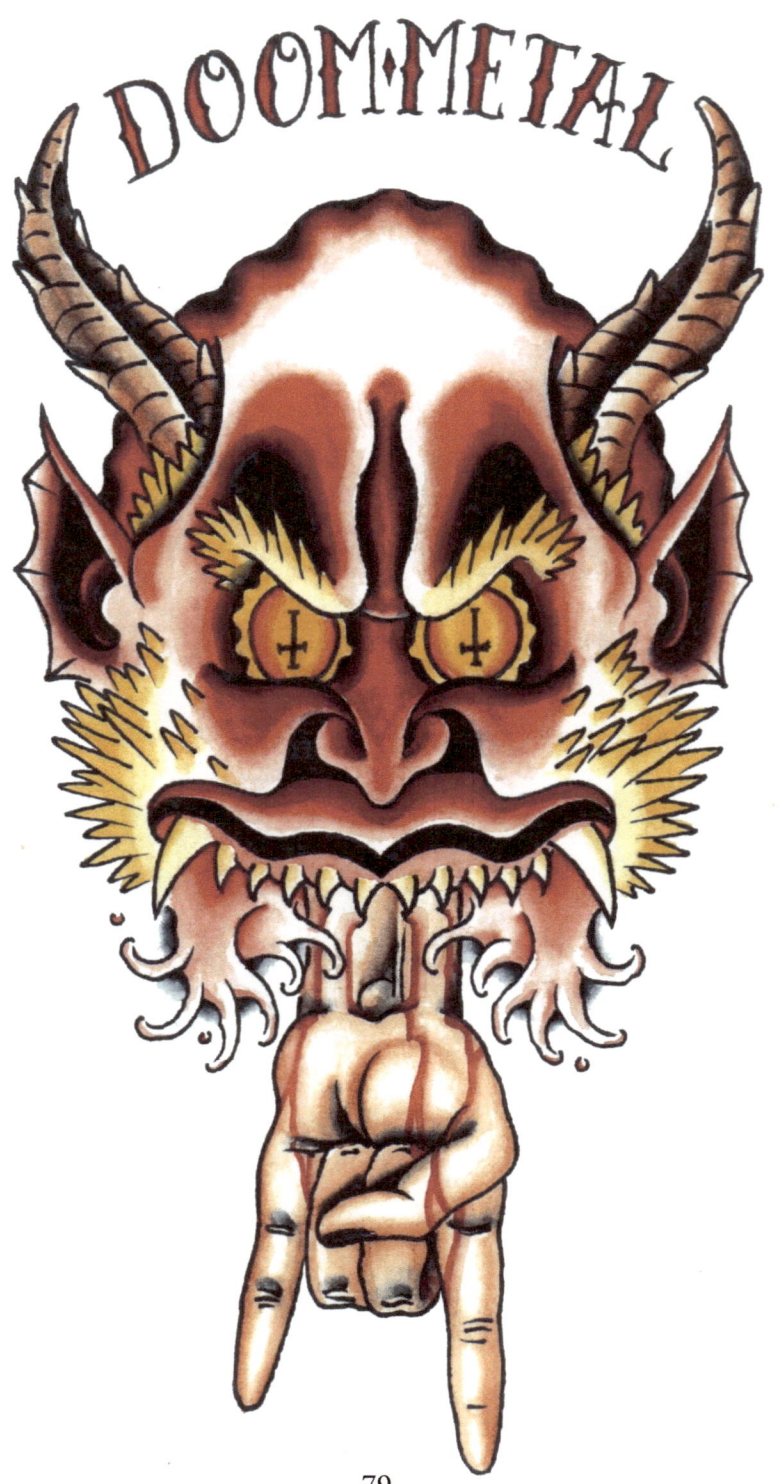

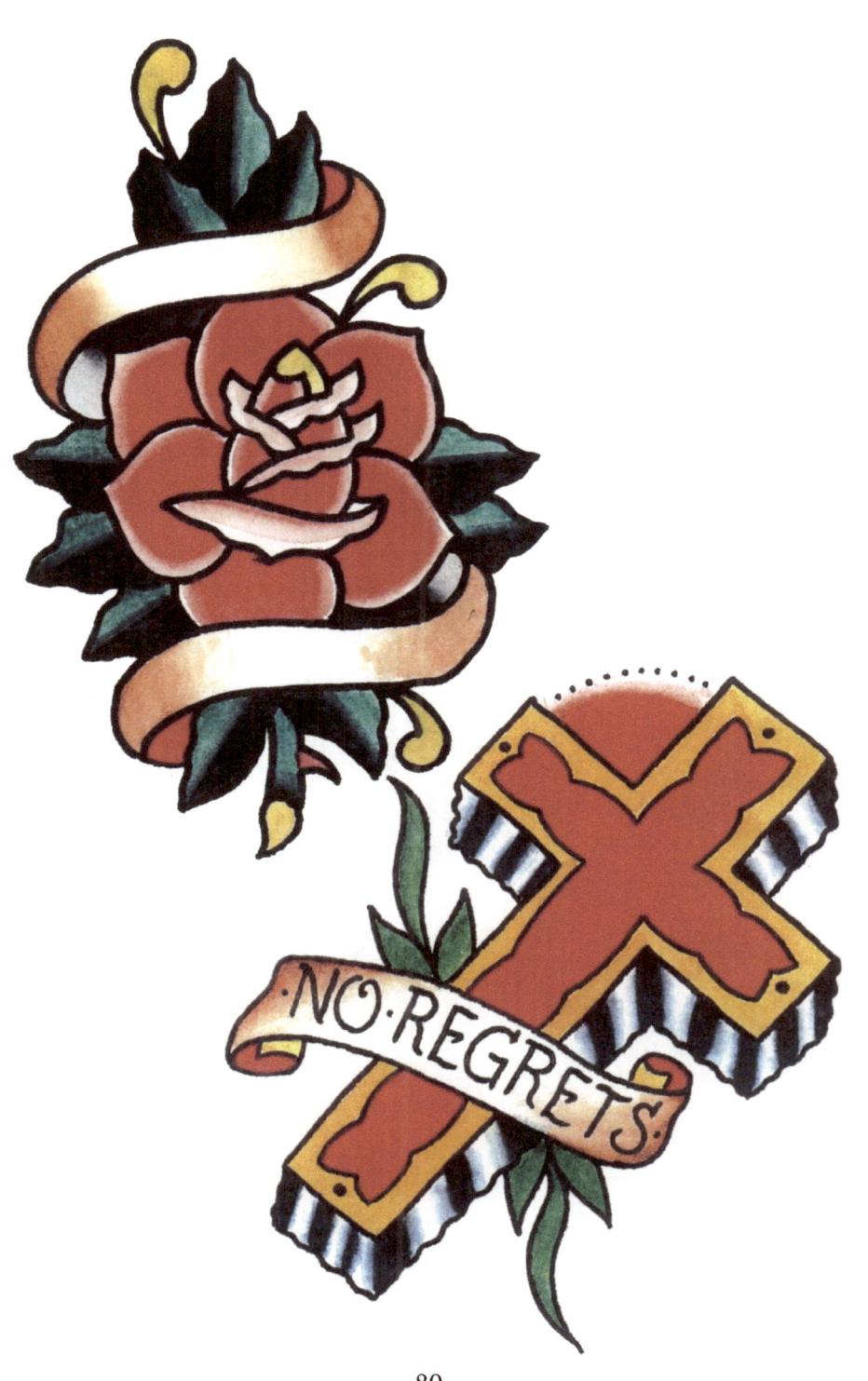

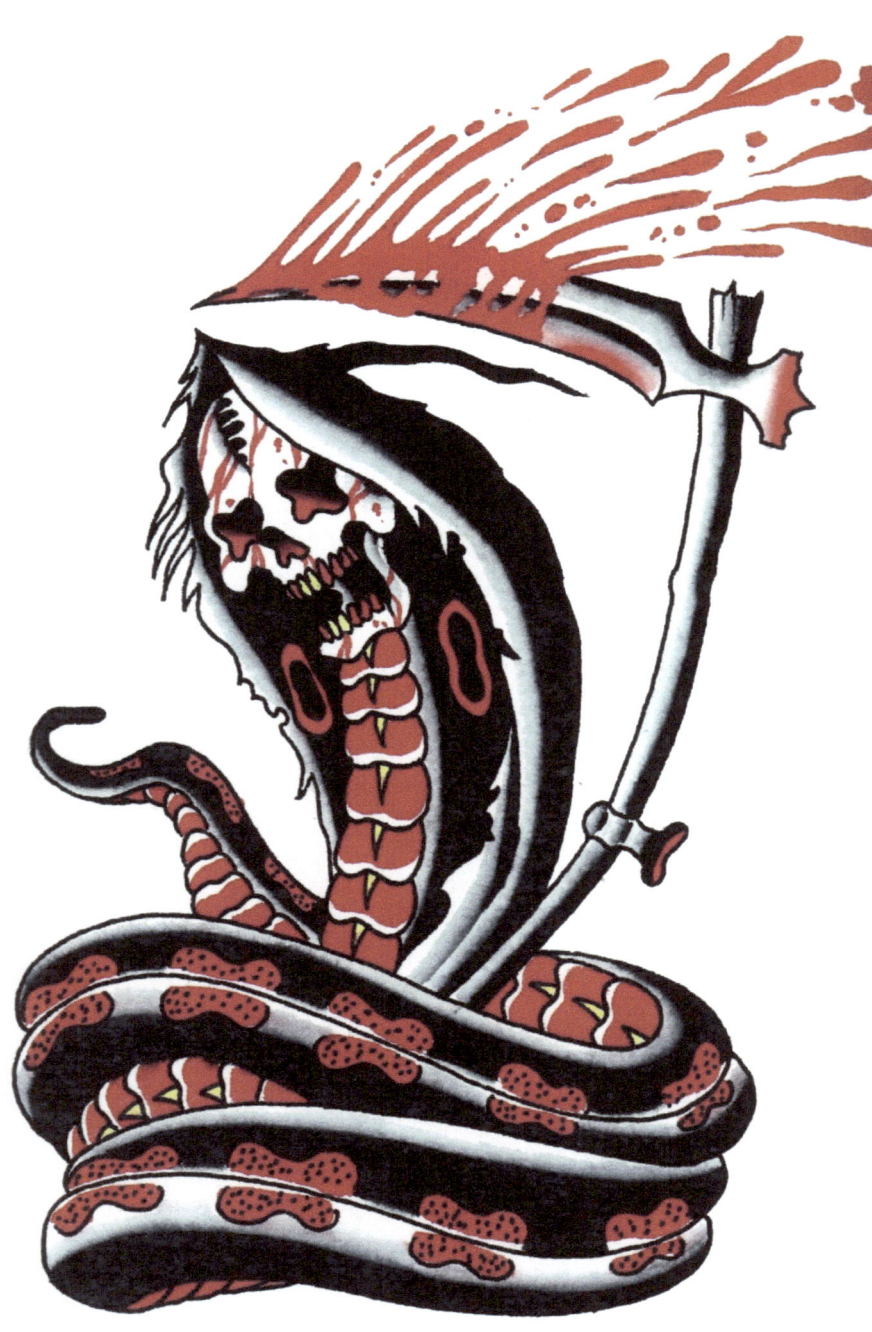

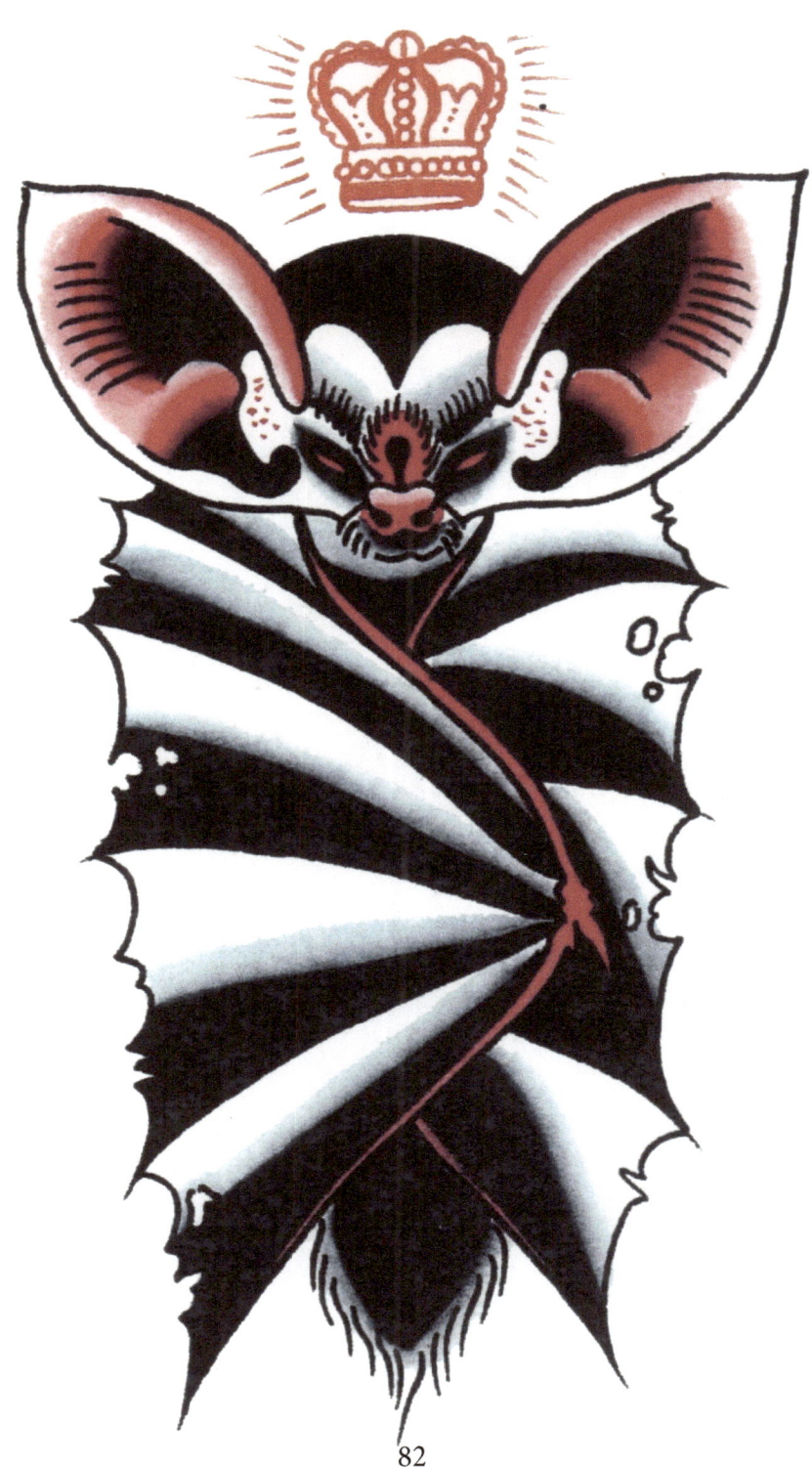

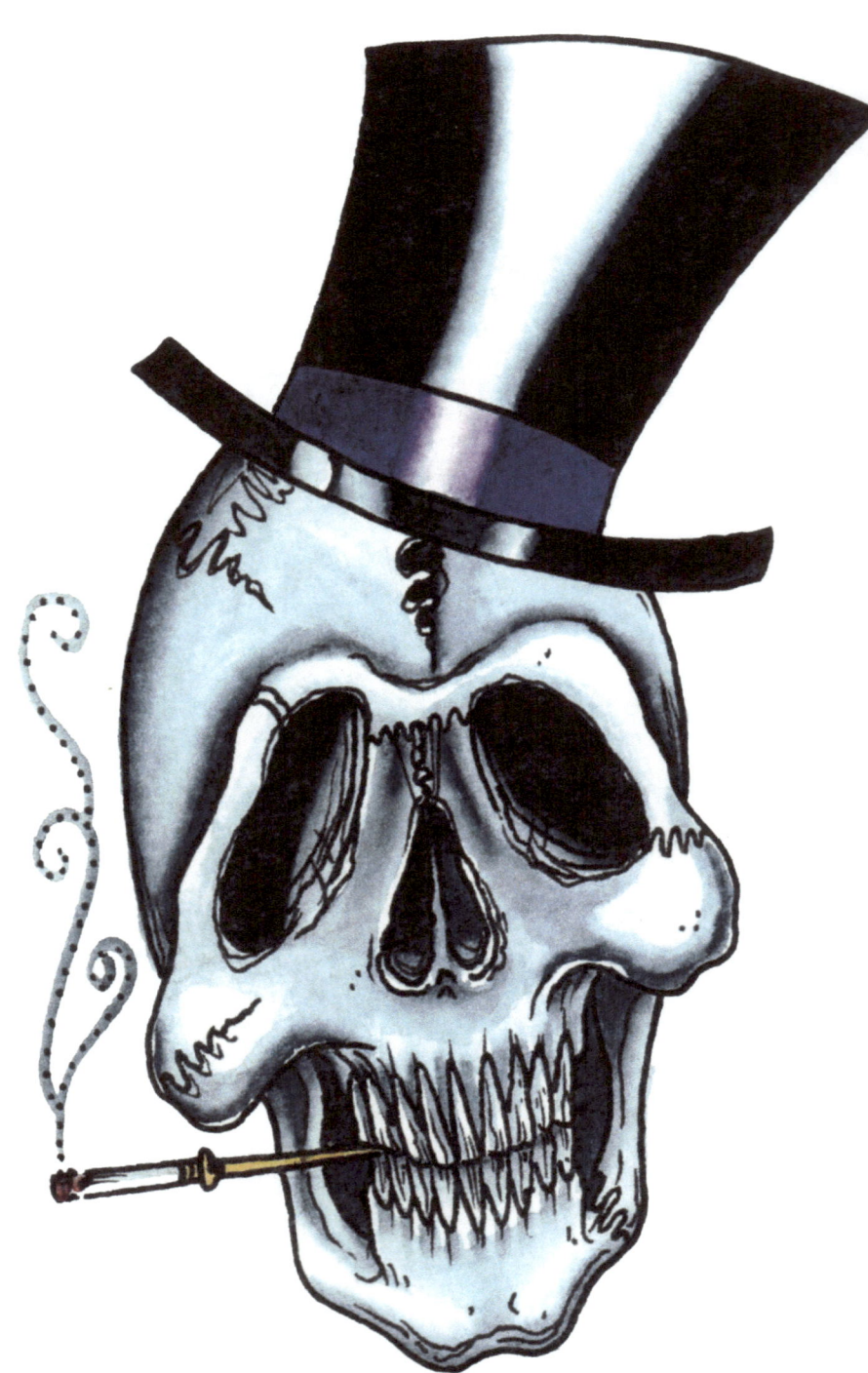

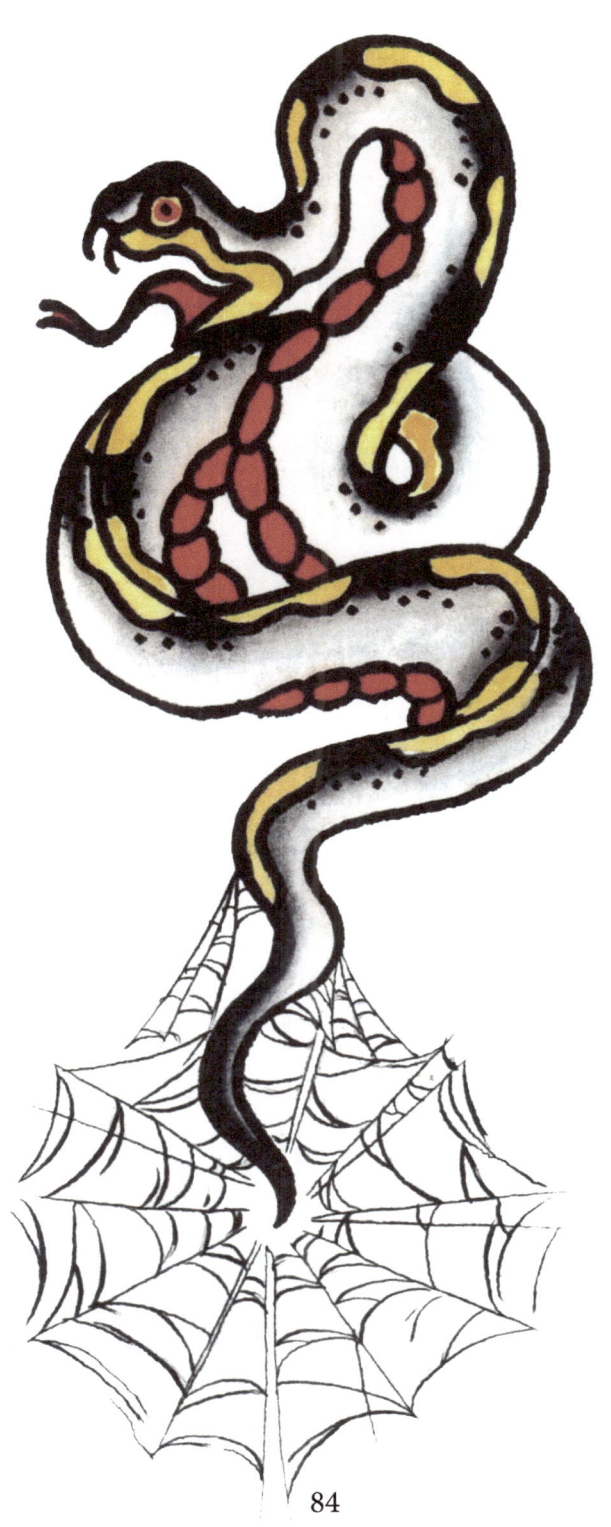

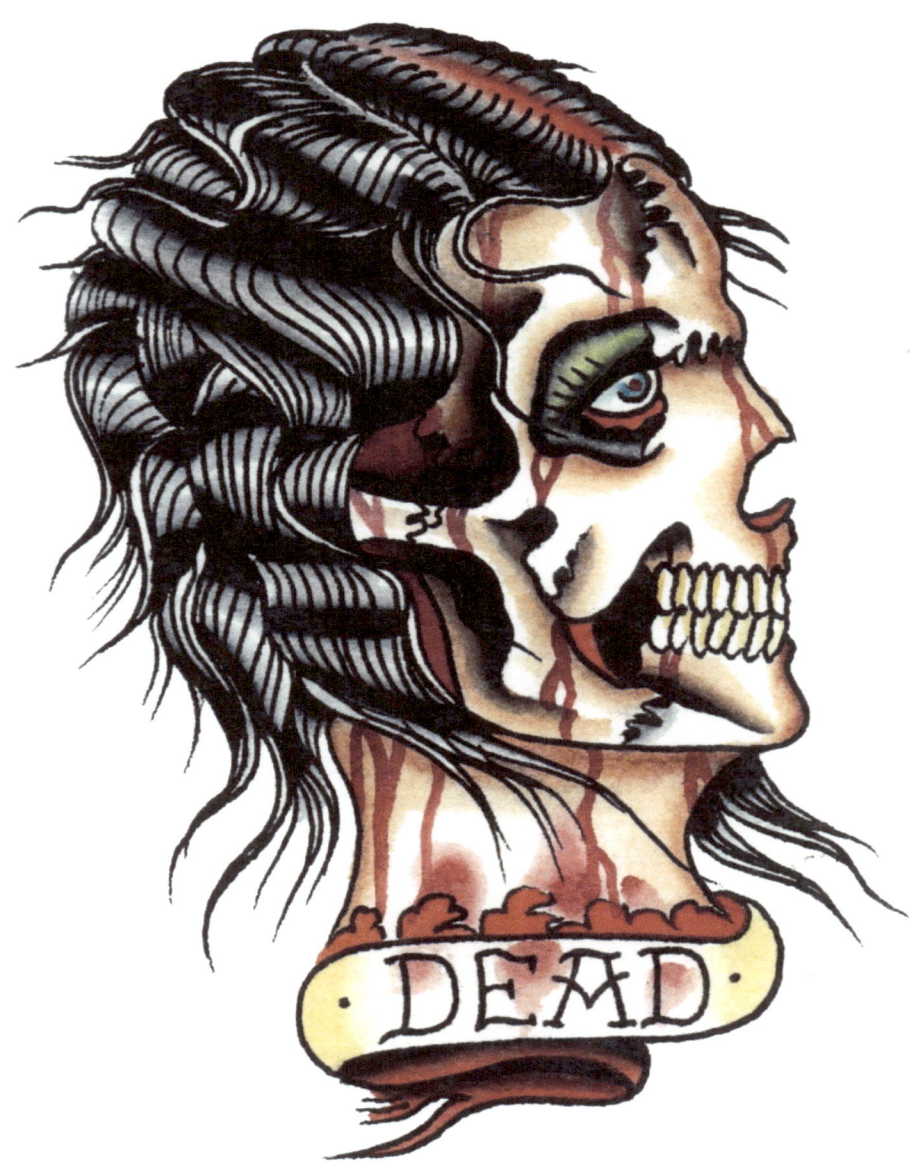

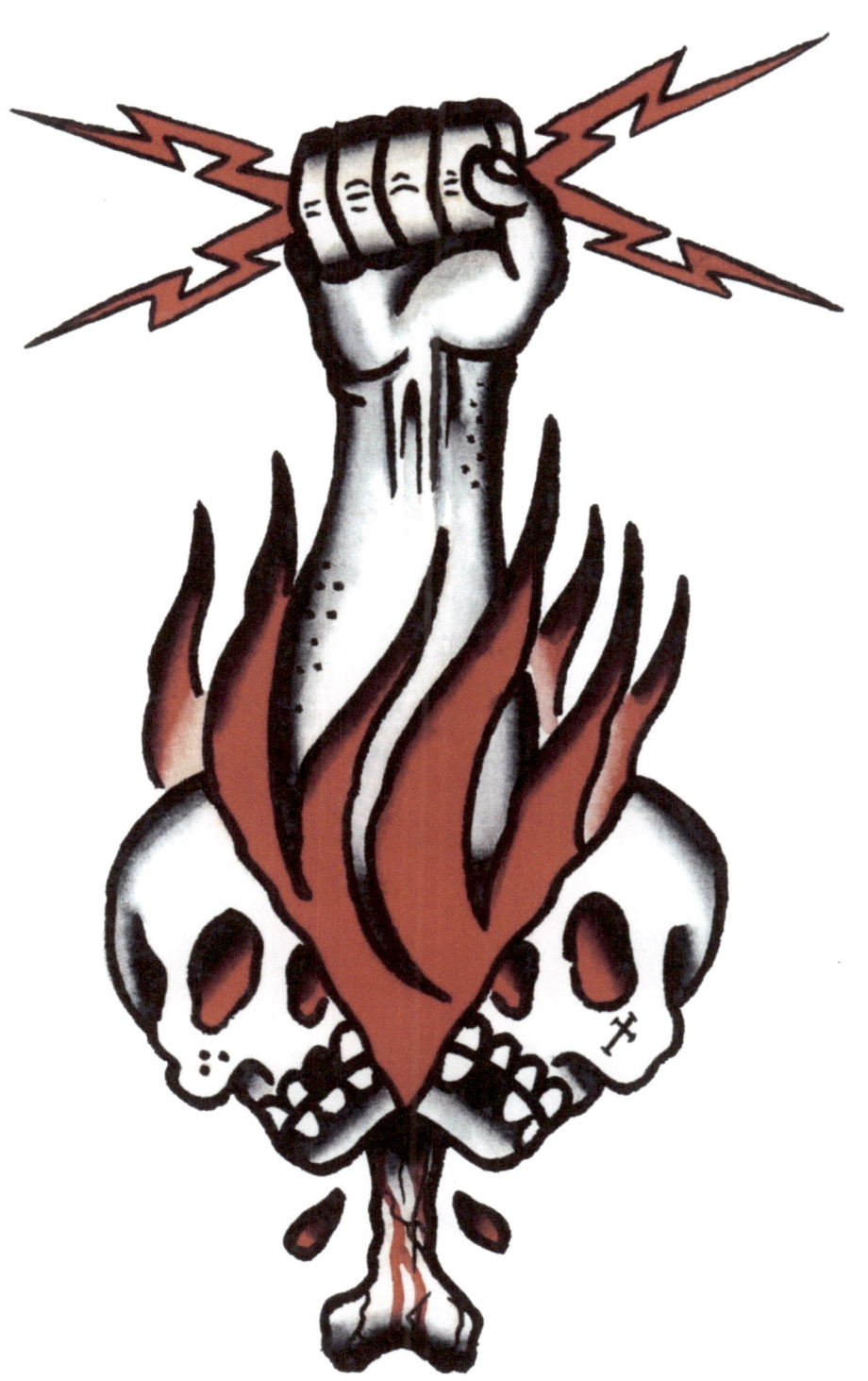

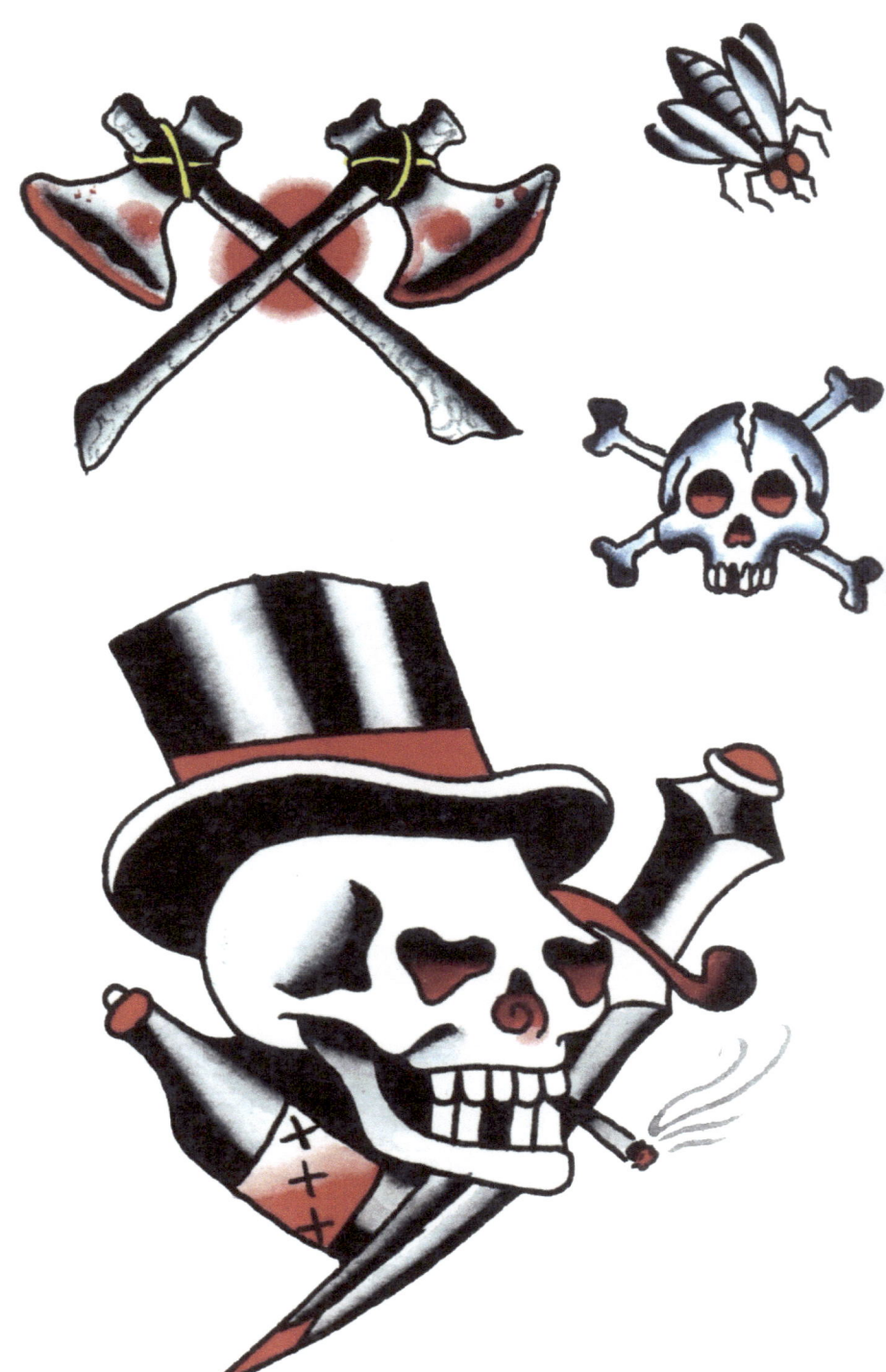

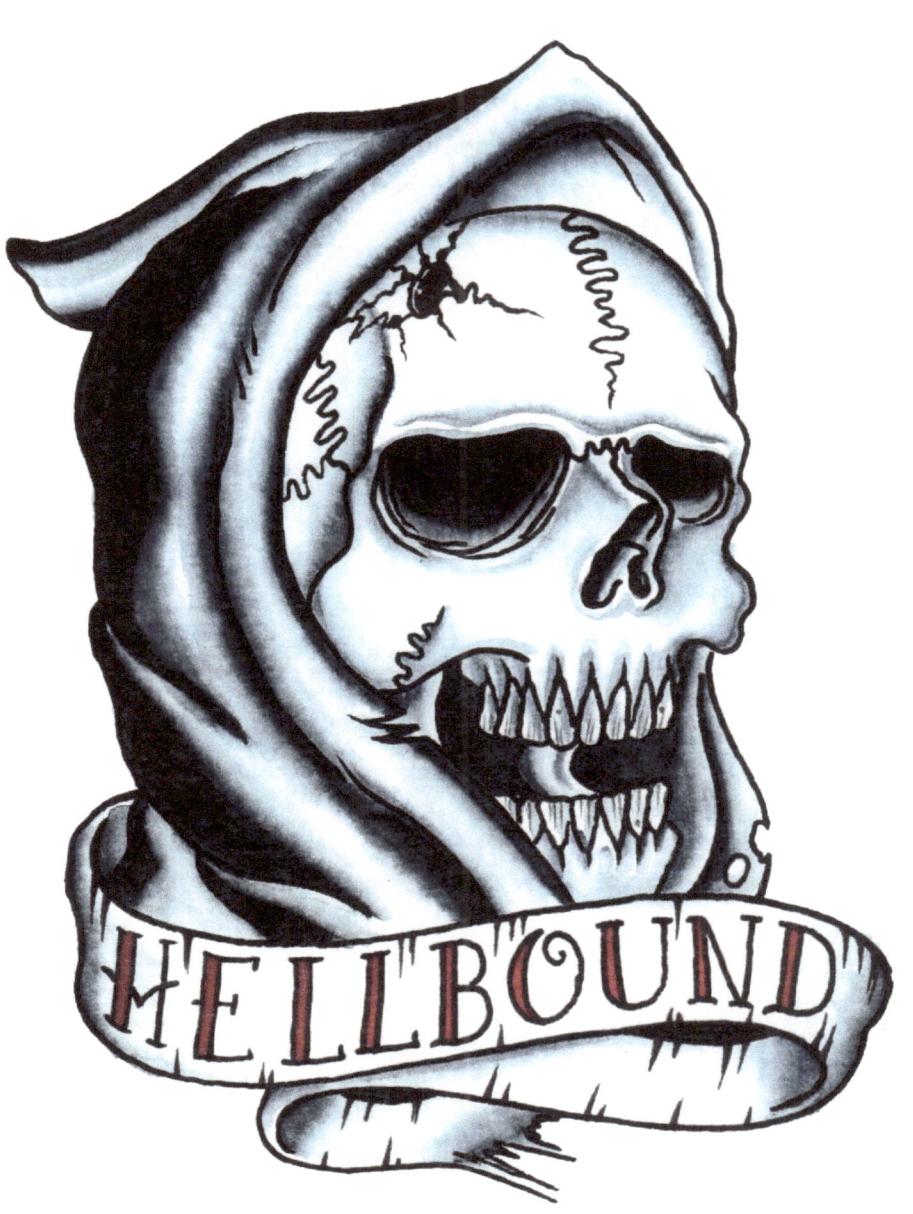

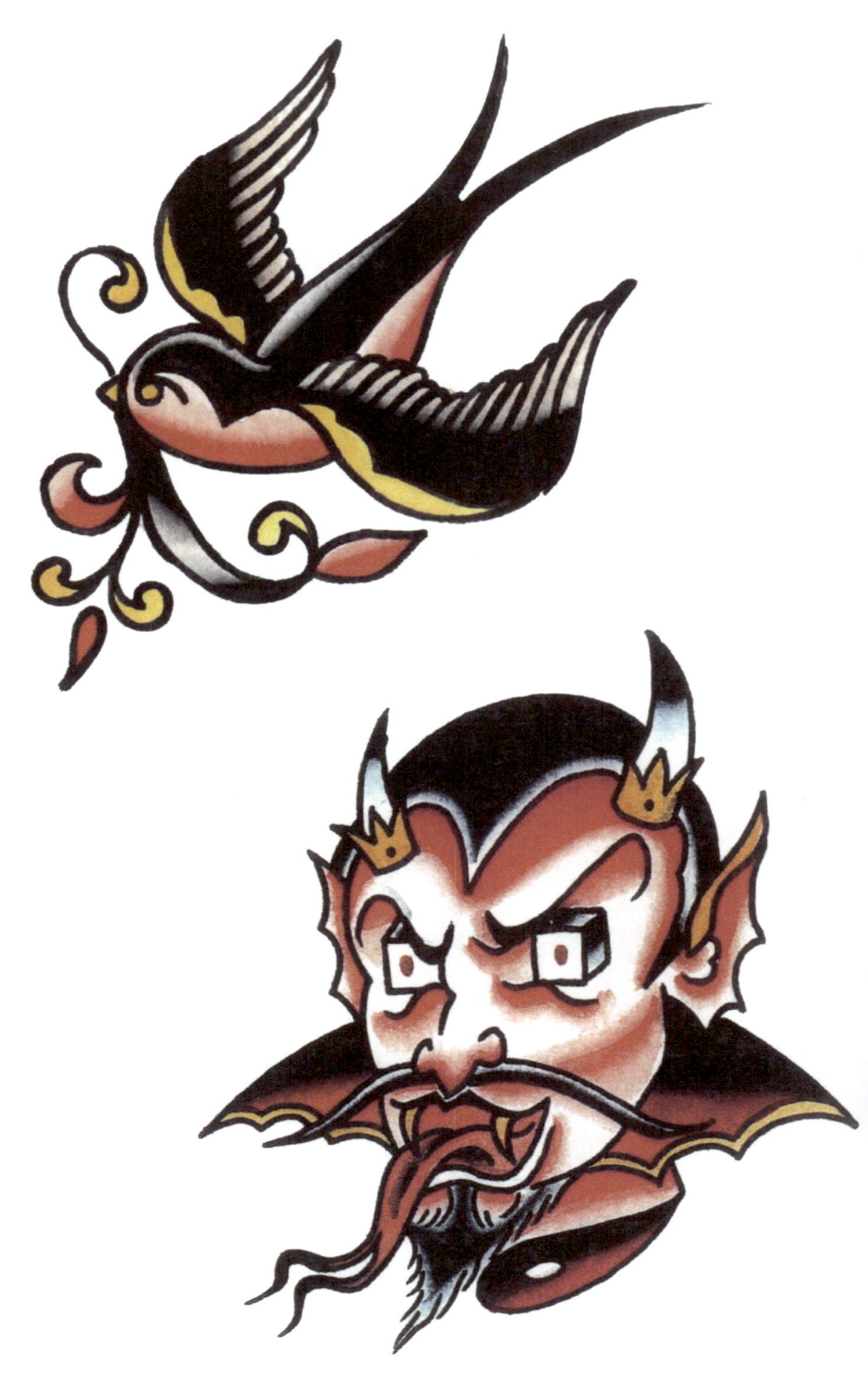

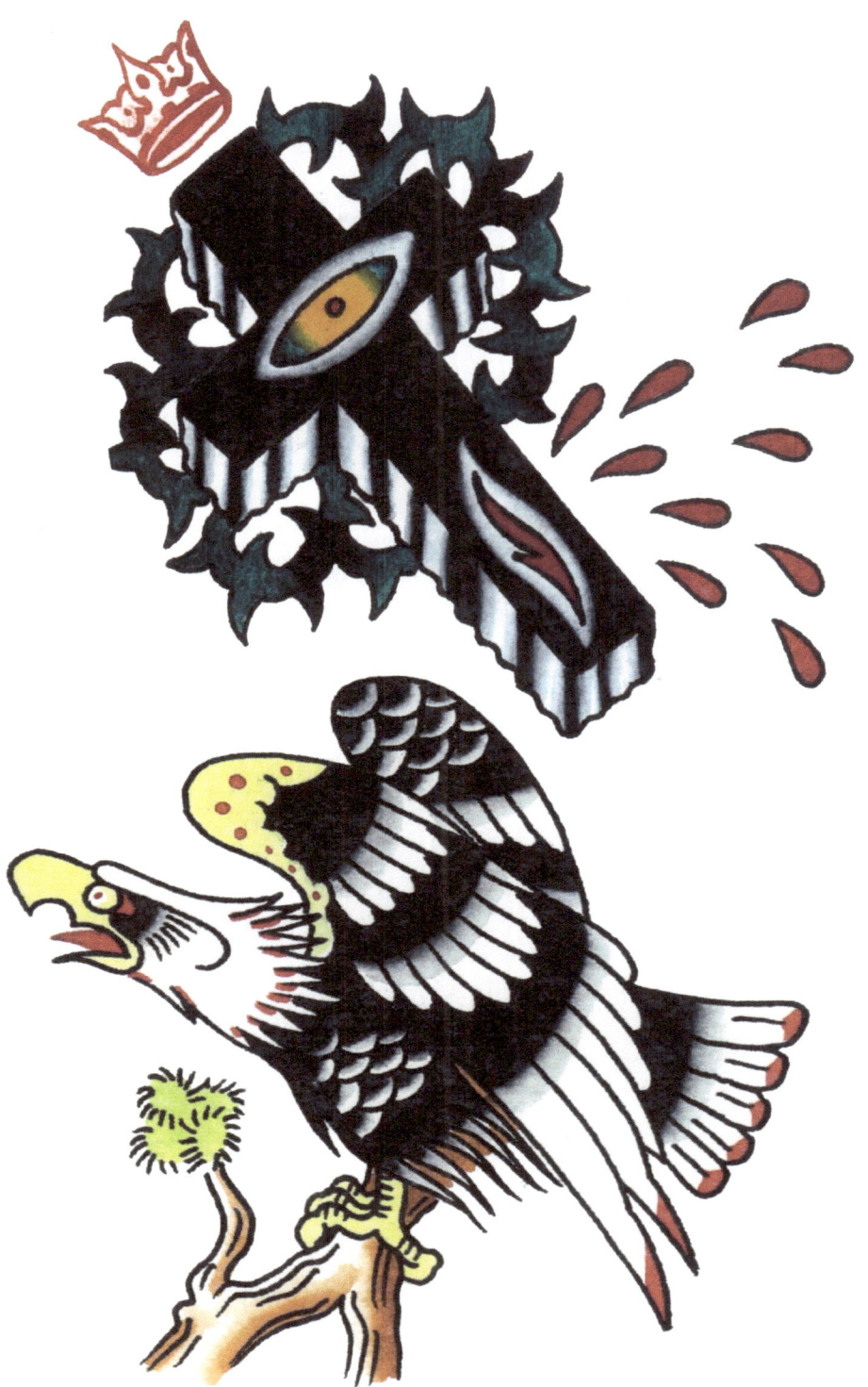

90

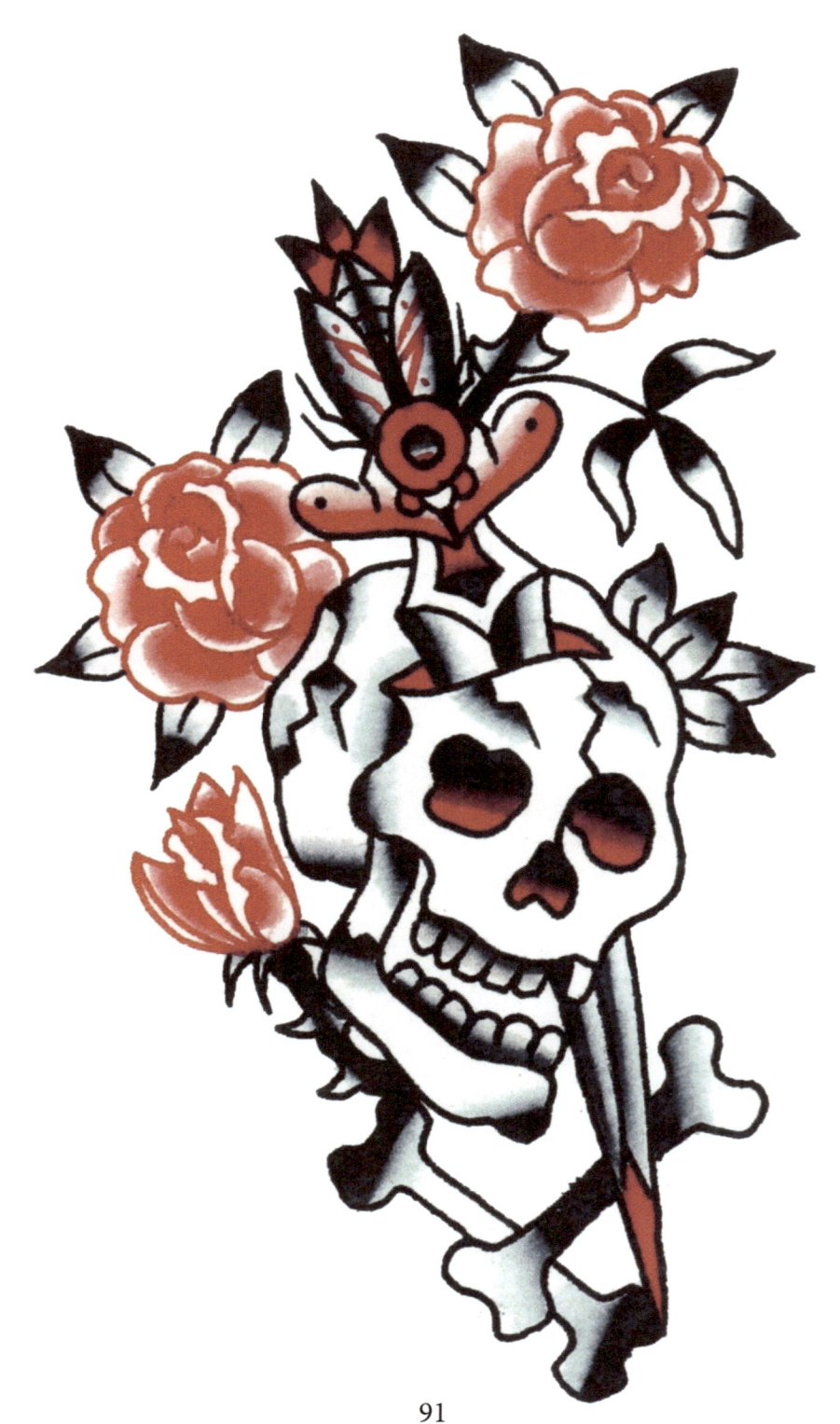

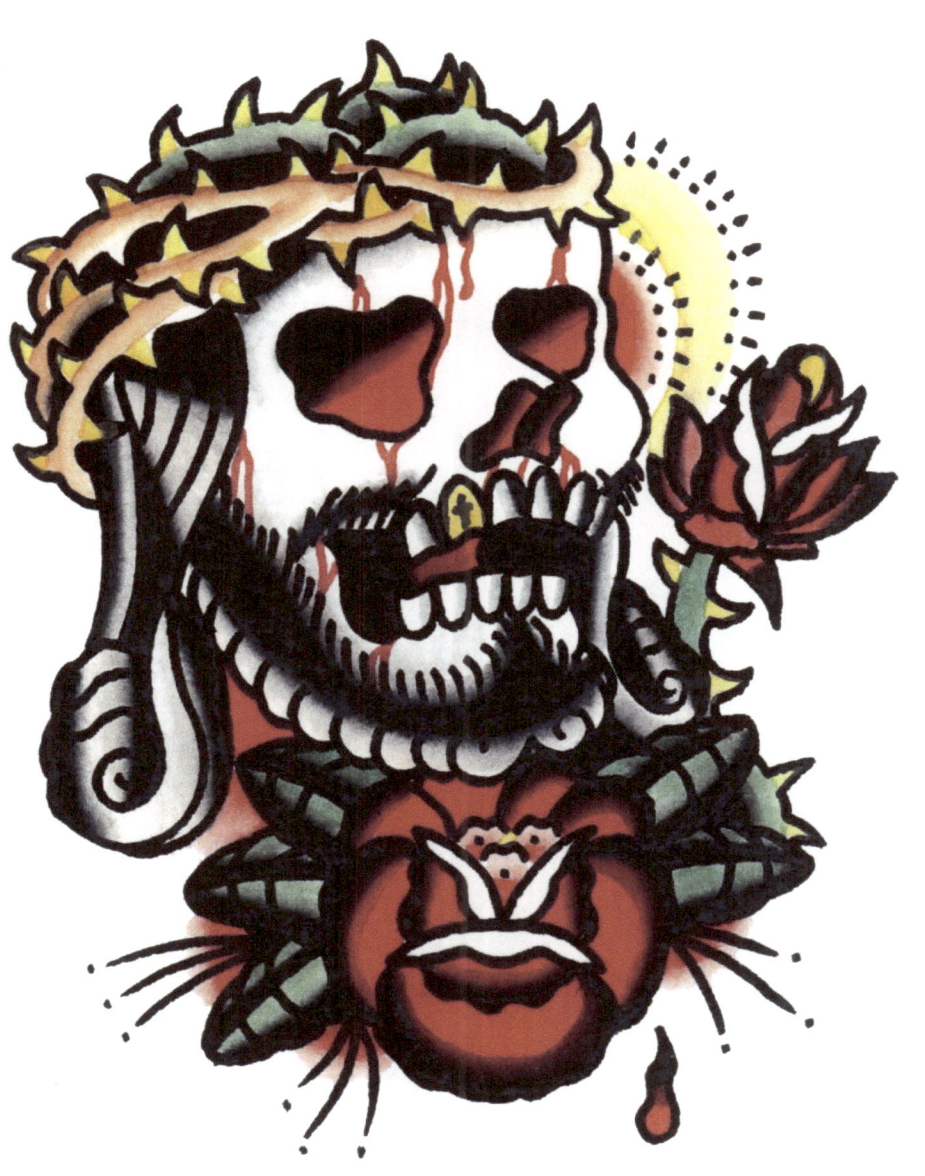

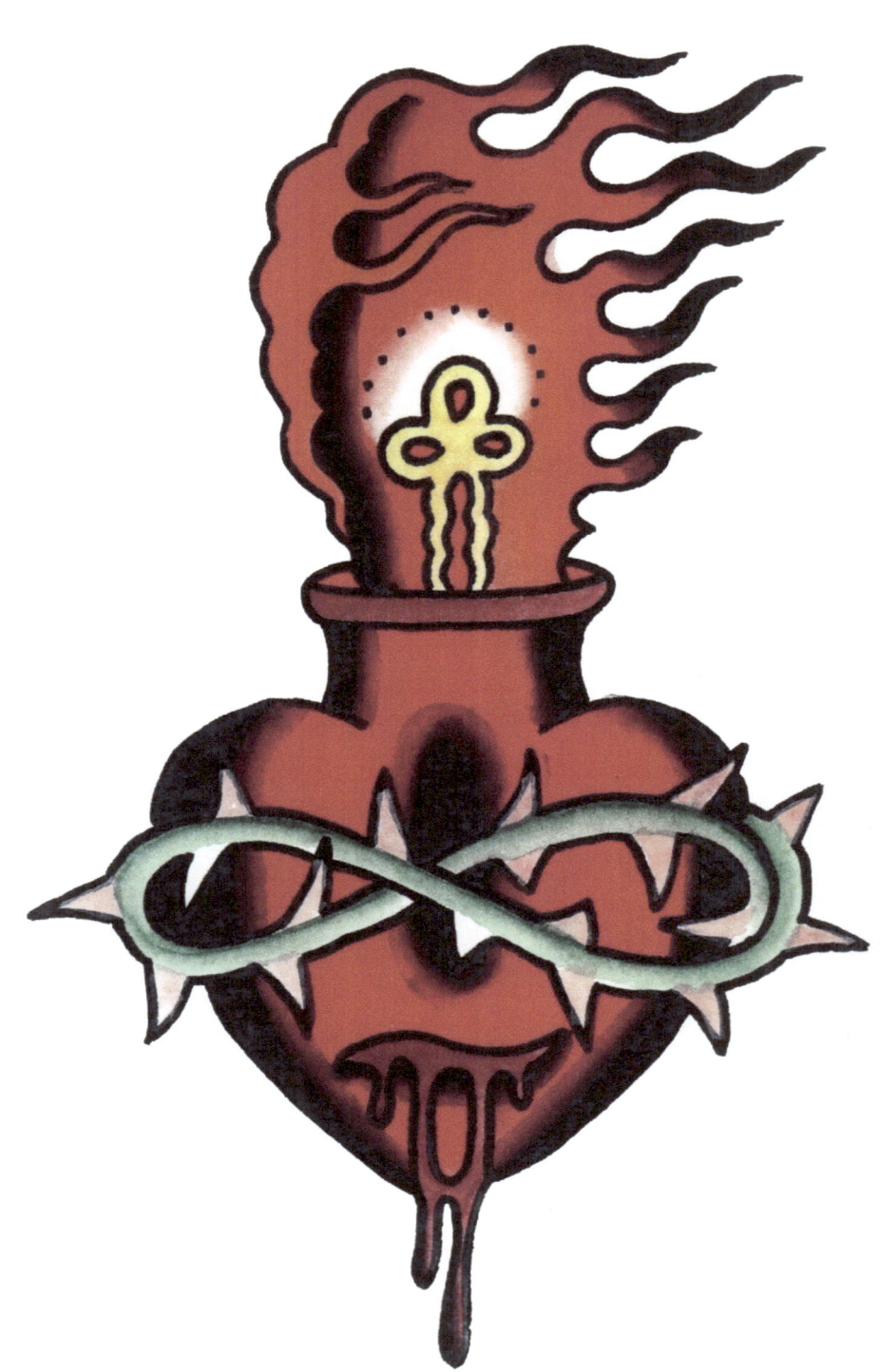

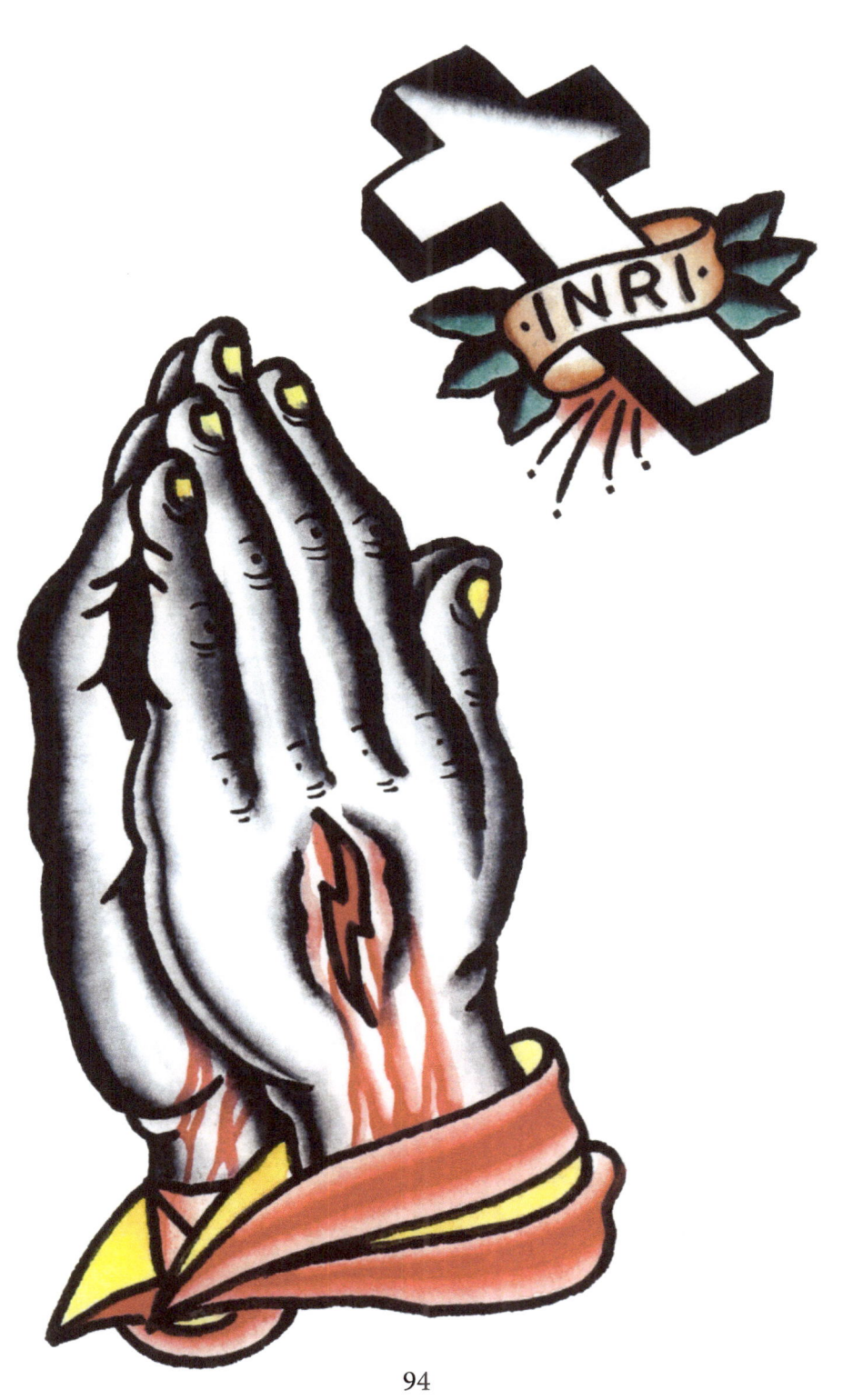

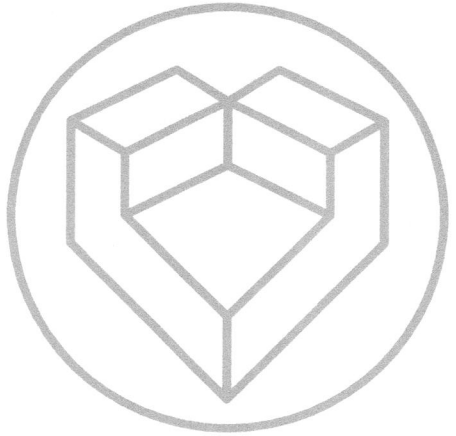

Adam Warmerdam
Dark Horse Tattoo
4644 Hollywood Blvd
Los Angeles, CA 90027
(323) 665-7345
darkhorsetattoola@gmail.
com

Adrian Sanchez
Apex Tattoo
4125 Piedmont Ave #5,
Oakland, CA 94611
(510) 858-5090

Andy Chism
Faith Tattoo
600 Mendocino Ave, Santa
Rosa, CA 95401
faithtattoo.ca
(707) 566-9955

Casey Cokrlic
Fine Line Tattoo
5510 Broadway Blvd, Gar-
land, TX 75043
(972) 240-0680

Chad Clark
Old Glory
Tattoos
12510 West Avenue, San
Antonio TX 78216
(210) 979-0802

Chance Kenyan
Jack Brown's Tattoo Re-
vival
1919 Princess Anne St,
Fredericksburg, VA 22401
(540) 899-9002

Derek Noble
Dark Age Tattoo
1205 E Pike St, Seattle,
WA 98122
(206) 323-1637

Dru Bias
Allegiance Tattoo
4716 E. Lake Highland Dr.
ste.110 The Colony, Texas
75056
 (469)353-8600

Greg Howell
Jack Brown's Tattoo Re-
vival
1919 Princess Anne St,
Fredericksburg, VA 22401
(540) 899-9002

Jason Freeman
Speakeasy Tattoo
150 Ridge Street
Reno, NV 89509
freemantattoo.com
(775) 502-5046

Jason Phillips
FTW Tattoo Parlor
6536 Telegraph Ave, Oakland, CA 94609
(510) 595-0389

Jef Wright
Coastline Tattoo
290A Commercial St.
Provincetown, MA 02657
(508) 487-2012

Jesse Haney
Avenue Tattoo
3020 Santa Rosa Ave ste F
Santa Rosa, CA 95407
(707) 544-8288

Jesse Swanson
Faith Tattoo
600 Mendocino Ave, Santa
Rosa, CA 95401
faithtattoo.ca
(707) 566-9955

Justin Shaw
Faith Tattoo
600 Mendocino Ave, Santa
Rosa, CA 95401
faithtattoo.ca
(707) 566-9955

Kenny Brown
Jack Brown's Tattoo Revival
1919 Princess Anne St,
Fredericksburg, VA 22401
(540) 899-9002

Nate Glomb
Faith Tattoo
600 Mendocino Ave, Santa
Rosa, CA 95401
(707) 566-9955

Nick Paine
Allied tattoo
48 1/2, Grattan Street,
Brooklyn, NY 11237
(347) 725-4861

RJ Hitchcock
American Tradition Tattoo
1219 19th St, Sacramento,
CA 95811
www.tatsacto.com
(916) 706-0734

Ryan Tanton
American Tradition Tattoo
1219 19th St, Sacramento,
CA 95811
www.tatsacto.com
(916) 706-0734

Sean Perkinson
FTW Tattoo Parlor
6536 Telegraph Ave, Oakland, CA 94609
(510) 595-0389

Steve Rieck
Collective Tattoo Parlor
8416 W Desert Inn Rd, Las Vegas, NV 89117
(702) 369-0718

Tyler Lunt
Speakeasy Tattoo
150 Ridge Street
Reno, NV 89509
lunttattoo.com

Walter McDonald
Lifetime Tattoo
1510 E Colfax Ave, Denver, CO 80218
lifetimetattoodenver.com
(303) 839-8088

Wesley Jackson
River City Tattoo
1028 2nd St, Sacramento, CA 95814
www.rivercitytattoo.net
(916) 448-1212

Wrath
American Tradition Tattoo
1219 19th St, Sacramento, CA 95811
www.tatsacto.com
(916) 706-0734

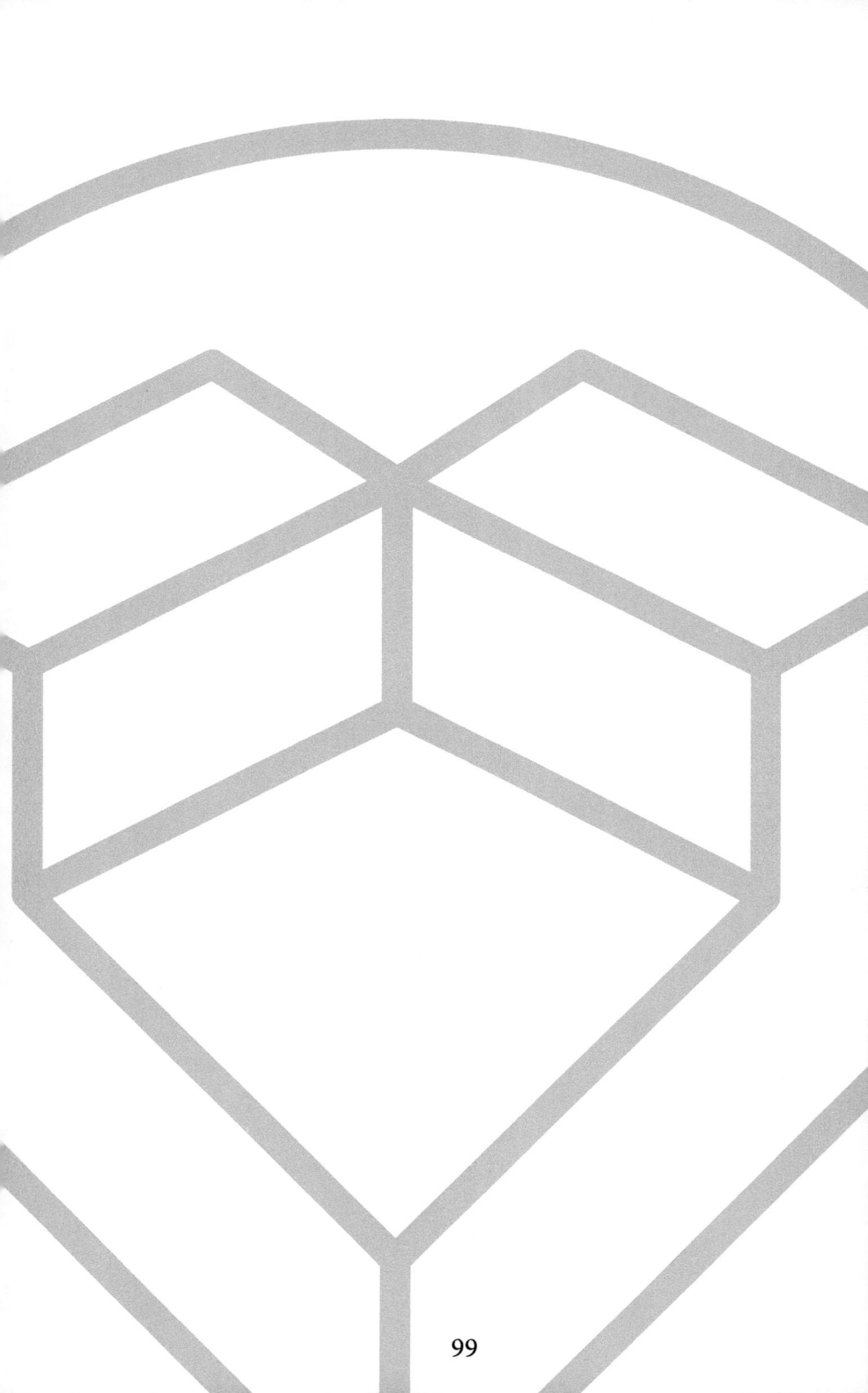

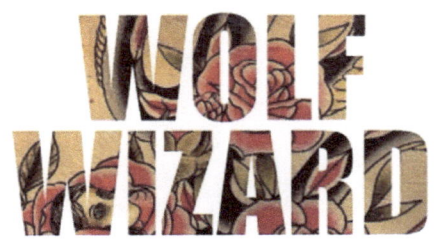